THINKING THROUGH LONELINESS

ALSO AVAILABLE FROM BLOOMSBURY

Prophetic Culture: Recreation for Adolescents, Federico Campagna
Political Philosophy in a Pandemic: Routes to a More Just Future, ed. Fay Niker and Aveek Bhattacharya
The Philosophy of Creative Solitudes, ed. David Jones
Enduring Time, Lisa Baraitser

THINKING THROUGH LONELINESS

DIANE ENNS

BLOOMSBURY ACADEMIC
LONDON • NEW YORK • OXFORD • NEW DELHI • SYDNEY

BLOOMSBURY ACADEMIC
Bloomsbury Publishing Plc
50 Bedford Square, London, WC1B 3DP, UK
1385 Broadway, New York, NY 10018, USA
29 Earlsfort Terrace, Dublin 2, Ireland

BLOOMSBURY, BLOOMSBURY ACADEMIC and the Diana logo are trademarks of Bloomsbury Publishing Plc

First published in Great Britain 2022

Copyright © Diane Enns, 2022

Diane Enns has asserted her right under the Copyright, Designs and Patents Act, 1988, to be identified as Author of this work.

For legal purposes the Acknowledgements on p. xii constitute an extension of this copyright page.

Cover design by Ben Anslow
Cover image: Frozen in Time © Lesley Oldaker

All rights reserved. No part of this publication may be reproduced or transmitted in any form or by any means, electronic or mechanical, including photocopying, recording, or any information storage or retrieval system, without prior permission in writing from the publishers.

Bloomsbury Publishing Plc does not have any control over, or responsibility for, any third-party websites referred to or in this book. All internet addresses given in this book were correct at the time of going to press. The author and publisher regret any inconvenience caused if addresses have changed or sites have ceased to exist, but can accept no responsibility for any such changes.

A catalogue record for this book is available from the British Library.

A catalog record for this book is available from the Library of Congress.

ISBN: HB: 978-1-3502-7973-5
PB: 978-1-3502-7974-2
ePDF: 978-1-3502-7975-9
eBook: 978-1-3502-7976-6

Typeset by Deanta Global Publishing Services, Chennai, India

To find out more about our authors and books visit www.bloomsbury.com and sign up for our newsletters.

For Brian Phillips

CONTENTS

Preface x
Acknowledgments xii

Part I What Is Loneliness? 1

The Paradox (I) 3

The Lonely I 4

The Lonely We 6

Stigma 8

In the Village 12

In the Loneliness Laboratory 14

The Paradox (II) 22

What Is Loneliness? 23

The Happiness of Others 29

The Alienation of Gregor Samsa 31

The Philosopher Stands Alone 33

In the Hole 43

The Ambivalence of Solitude 45

Solus 56

Alone Together 59

Part II Why Are We Lonely? 63

"Organized Loneliness" 65

The Tyranny of the Couple 71

At Home 80

The Antisocial Family 82

Against Community 89

Nostalgia 97

"The Soul at Work" 100

In the Desert 112

The Iron Band of Technology 116

Social Failure 124

Part III What Do We Need? 129

Pandemic Pause 131

To Belong 138

Proximity 141

Distance 144

In the Neighborhood 147

At the Café 151

At the Market 155

CONTENTS

    Care 157

    Friendship 161

    Love 164

    The Join 166

    Witness 168

Notes 169
Bibliography 188
Index 197

PREFACE

This is a book of reflections on loneliness—on how it feels, what it means, why we experience it, and what it tells us about human social life. My intent is to understand this particular form of suffering, not to provide advice on how to overcome it. In the pages that follow, I attempt to think through loneliness in the double sense this phrase implies: applying my mind to the subject of loneliness in a sustained way, and drawing out insights we may only discover through the experience of loneliness.

I wouldn't know how to explore a phenomenon as profound and complex as loneliness in the abstract; my own experiences are the starting points of all questions and considerations, invitations to readers to discover their own starting points. As with any type of human suffering, loneliness is subjective. We may be able to say to an author—*yes, this is what loneliness feels like*—but the intensity and duration of the distress, its conditions and our ability to cope with it, vary considerably. At the same time, loneliness is a fundamental human experience with objective conditions. My hope is that the descriptions and analyses in this book will resonate with its readers and provoke them to further reflect on human social needs and what happens when they are not met.

Most of this book was written before the start of a global pandemic that has intensified public discussions of loneliness—discussions that referred to a looming social crisis long before we ever uttered the phrase "social distancing." As I was completing the last part of the manuscript in the early months of the first lockdown in my city, I was gripped by the feeling that everything needed to be rewritten in light of this colossal event. The coronavirus divided time and what came before it now seemed to belong to a distant era. I resisted the temptation to alter what I had already completed, however, though I added occasional

PREFACE

references to the pandemic and some reflections on the effects of those early months of what can only be described as social shock. The isolation necessitated by the pandemic has highlighted many of the vexing issues discussed in this book. After hearing some residents of care homes tell us they would prefer to die of the virus than continue to be prohibited from seeing their loved ones, can we treat loneliness as a personal affliction and ignore its origins in social failure? Technology may have saved those of us who work from home, or who live alone, but how will we resist the further inflation of its power over us? What will happen to our conception of home if it doubles as the workplace, to our public spaces when offices are abandoned, to the employees who live alone and must now work alone as well? Will we continue to adjust to disembodied connections, finding ever novel ways to mask the symptoms of our collective loneliness? No one has answers to these questions; we only know that contemporary social life is in upheaval.

Arundhati Roy calls the pandemic "a portal, a gateway from one world to the next." Despite the global economic and political failures she tirelessly exposes to the public, Roy is hopeful that this particular rupture in time will inspire us to imagine and fight for a different world.[1] I think of this as I walk through the parks in my city, which a pandemic winter has transformed into public spaces more vibrant than I can remember from past years. Clusters of friends and families dot the vast soccer fields, or circle fire pits, sharing picnics or barbecue, dogs and Frisbees; the only sound is the wind in the trees, and the musical rise and fall of conversation and laughter. We must not forget what a joyous surprise it was to rediscover—after painful deprivation—how indispensable we are to one another.

ACKNOWLEDGMENTS

I am indebted to all the students, colleagues, friends, and strangers with whom I've had conversations about loneliness over the last few years. Particular thanks go to five philosophy students at Ryerson University who diligently hunted down sources, helped prepare the manuscript, and discussed all the conditions and effects of loneliness with me: Jordan DeJonge, Jan Wozniak, Connor MacCaulay, Jenna Beehler, and John Czafit. For her meticulous editing and thoughtful engagement with all the ideas in this book, I express my deepest appreciation to my sister, Karen Enns, without whom the creative process would be lonelier than it has to be.

I would also like to acknowledge the Social Sciences and Humanities Research Council of Canada for funding my research project on loneliness and the Banff Centre for Arts and Creativity for supporting a month of writing in a spectacular mountain setting—the stuff of dreams for this Toronto resident. At Bloomsbury Press, Liza Thompson and Lucy Russell were marvelous to work with—ever efficient, good-humored and resourceful. I am grateful to three anonymous reviewers for their generous and thoughtful comments. A special thank you to Antonio Calcagno for his unflagging support of my work, and for those summer days of thinking and writing together in our beloved Toronto libraries.

Some material from "'Organized Loneliness,'" "'The Soul at Work,'" and "The Iron Band of Technology" was previously published as "Organized Loneliness" in *Tropos: Journal of Hermeneutics and Philosophical Criticism*, vol. 1, 2019. I would like to thank the editor, Gaetano Chiurazzi, for kindly granting permission to reprint.

I dedicate this book to Brian Phillips, in honor of the immeasurable gifts of his friendship and passion for thinking.

PART I
WHAT IS LONELINESS?

THE PARADOX (I)

Across the street from London's Tate Britain sits an unusual public toilet, the creation of Italian-born artist Monica Bonvicini. It began as an art installation in 2004, inspired by Bonvicini's observations of guests at art show openings who don't want to miss a moment of the event, not because they are keen to see the art, but because they hate to miss the spectacle of the opening—the grand entrances, free drinks, gossip, and ceremony.[1]

The installation, called "Don't Miss a Sec," promises users of this facility they won't have to miss a thing. The fully functional toilet is housed in a structure made with different types of glass that when combined approximate a one-way mirrored surface.[2] No one on the street can see inside the cubicle, but for any of the toilet's occupants, life passes by with alarming clarity. Viewers might wonder whether anyone brave enough to use the facilities would feel exposed anyway, as though they were carrying out their most private function in public.

When I am most lonely, I feel as though I am trapped inside Bonvicini's installation. I am separated from the world, watching it spin by from an impassable distance. I can see everyone, but no one can see me. Even if they glance at the mirrored wall as they stride by my glass prison and I meet their gazes full on, they see only their own images. I am not missing anything, though I am not actually present.

This is the peculiar paradox of loneliness: I am unseen yet I feel exposed, as though my most internal suffering were on public display, as though I am disclosing to the world the vulnerability it does not want to see.

THE LONELY I

To retain the I when writing of loneliness is a struggle. While we can find eloquent accounts of loneliness in the first person, it is rare to find a writer who describes loneliness while they are actually feeling lonely. Olivia Laing begins *The Lonely City* by relating her "not so long ago" experience of loneliness after moving to New York City for a man who promptly ends their relationship. Emily White ruminates on an intense "chronic" loneliness only after she has fallen in love. Thomas Dumm analyzes loneliness looking back on a period of grief over the death of his wife.[1] The more scholarly the analysis, the more hidden the I. If the authors of sociological or psychological studies of loneliness are lonely, we would never know it.

There are exceptions. The American psychologist Clark Moustakas writes poignantly about discovering loneliness as a fact of the human condition only once he had to decide with his wife whether to proceed with a high-risk surgery for their five-year-old daughter. He does not spare the reader; we are exposed to his vulnerability and invited to experience with him the feelings of terror and aloneness engendered by his responsibility for another's life. The most intense feelings arise when Moustakas witnesses his daughter's seizures after surgery; her abject aloneness and his abject helplessness instill in him what he calls an "indescribable loneliness."[2]

The I never retreats in Moustakas's account; the present tense does not slide definitively into the past. He discloses his own loneliness without flinching, describing himself as a "solitary, isolated, lonely individual."[3] This I is his access point to the suffering of others.

The lonely I discloses itself more freely now that we have the limitless space of a virtual universe inviting self-display. Anyone can contribute their "deeply personal yet profoundly universal" stories to

"The Loneliness Project," for example, a site that assures us we are never alone and promises the power to heal.[4] But the anonymous I of the internet is disembodied and narcissistic, its sentiments one-dimensional, as inaccessible as the hidden I.

To speak of the lonely I risks exacerbating the very conditions that give rise to it. I recently shared something of my own history of loneliness during an interview on a radio program. I spoke of significant periods of isolation and alienation—as a single mother in my late twenties and early thirties, after an impossible intimate relationship in my forties, and at my workplace in my early fifties. I mentioned the curious reactions of others when broaching the subject of loneliness; for example, the unease of my teaching assistants when I taught a unit on loneliness in a philosophy course and expected them to discuss the topic with their students. Once the interview was over, my host confessed that he, too, felt a little "strange" after our discussion. I winced at this, alone in the soundproof cubicle of my local radio station, overcome by the desire to protest—but I'm not lonely now![5]

I want to reiterate this protest every time I tell someone I am writing about loneliness. To speak of it is rather like divulging one has cancer— better to mention it after it's gone.

THE LONELY WE

I first wrote about loneliness while attending a summer program in literary journalism. I didn't know much about the genre, but the "literary" promised freedom from the scholarly constraints of academic writing. I imagined finding my people—wordsmiths, lovers of metaphor.

Every morning I withdrew to a tiny cabin in the Canadian Rockies with only trees, birds, and the occasional deer for company. My aloneness there was not painful but pleasurable. The air was still, and the silence and solitude were essential for thinking. Time slipped by unnoticed. I was Thoreau at Walden Pond, writing of solitude, his best companion.

But whenever I left this idyll to return to the group, I was overcome by loneliness. My fellow writers may have been wordsmiths, but I was an alien among them. I did not need to make my living from writing as they did—an enviable freedom. The reflective nature of my project was not popular; I was interested in the ideas below the surface of a story rather than the details of the story itself. I was not privy to the mechanics of journalism. *Use direct, Anglo-Saxon words*, the program director would bellow at me as he crossed out "alleviate" and wrote "lifted." I was not angry or funny enough and failed to describe details like the coffee my narrator was drinking—this is what the reader wants, I was instructed. To make matters worse, I was much older than my fellow participants and enjoyed the pleasures of sleep and sobriety rather more than they did.

But perhaps my greatest offense was disclosing the lonely I and tracing its implications for the lonely we. I wanted to understand loneliness in all of its ambiguity—as part of the human condition and as socially conditioned. I wanted my own explorations to be a gateway to understanding how others experience loneliness. To this end, I attempted a fluid move from I to we, inviting the reader to think with me. But my use of we was met with resistance, even hostility. I was accused of alienating the reader, a response I found baffling. Others had been cheered for their stories of personal suffering and rebellion and obsession, but my exposure seemed exceptional.

I realized they wanted me to be lonely all by myself.

STIGMA

The admission of "strange" feelings after listening to someone talk of loneliness evokes something a shade darker than discomfort, perhaps captured in Freud's essay "The Uncanny." "Uncanny" is a rough translation of the German *unheimlich*, which is the opposite of *heimlich* or "home," terms that turn out to be ambiguously joined. Freud reviews historical definitions of heimlich that evoke the comforts and familiarity of one's home, the tranquility of a private space, and refer to what is concealed and secretive. Unheimlich or uncanny feelings arise when we feel like strangers or foreigners, when we are not at ease as we would be in our familiar surroundings. Freud, of course, relates this uneasiness to sexual matters, to the fear of castration, or to the anxiety in neurotic men, caused by the sight of women's genitals. The latter point supports his observation that the meaning of heimlich alludes to comfort and familiarity, as well as to anxiety over what is hidden (everyone's first home—the womb) and in this way heimlich slips into unheimlich.[1] An uncanny feeling arises when we encounter something familiar yet repressed, Freud concludes, quoting an illuminating line by Friedrich Schelling: "'Unheimlich' *is the name for everything that ought to have remained . . . secret and hidden but has come to light.*"[2]

    I am not about to relate loneliness to the horror of women's genitals (though who really knows?), but I would like to suggest encountering another's loneliness produces uneasy feelings because it reminds us of a condition we would like to forget—our essential vulnerability. Schelling's point is relevant here—the strange feelings evoked by another's admission of loneliness are caused by what "ought to remain hidden" or, at least, what we would like to remain hidden. The lonely person reminds others of their own essential or potential aloneness, a reminder that goes a long way to explain the stigma of loneliness.

Perhaps loneliness reminds us of the absolute aloneness of death, which is the culminating point of our vulnerability.

Quite simply, human beings are vulnerable because we are mortal. The Latin origin of the term "vulnerable" is *vulnerare*, which means to wound.[3] To accept our vulnerability is to accept our relative powerlessness, our woundability, under even the most banal life circumstances. When a lonely person speaks of his suffering, his vulnerability provokes a spectrum of responses—empathy in some, while discomfort, hostility, or even rage in others. The more we fear our own vulnerability, the more intolerable we may find another's.

There are parallels in our encounters with another's grief. A common response to an expression of grief is avoidance. Surprisingly, such a response can lead to isolating the mourner, the very opposite of what most grieving people need. Coupled friends may no longer invite the widow to their gatherings or outings. Acquaintances feel so awkward in the presence of a grieving person that they do not ask about the lost loved one or invite the mourner to talk about her sorrow. Even close friends can be inexplicably unavailable when we are in mourning.

What grief and loneliness have in common: they remind us that we are all unequivocally vulnerable to loss and death; they loudly proclaim our need for one another. When we lose a well-loved person a part of us also dies, the unique part created and nurtured together with the one we loved, a dynamic between two that we can never replicate with another. We fight the death of this part of us through remembering, keeping the person alive in conversation and in our cherished collection of his things—a watch or sweater, his books and letters.

An uncanny response to loneliness helps us understand its stigma, the perception that the lonely person is dogged by "some pariah aura of untouchability or sickness," as Rollo May puts it.[4] We fear the lonely and the grieving are contagious; they will spread the germs of loneliness and remind us of our mortality.

But at a certain point the analogy with grief breaks apart. The shame of loneliness renders its stigma more than a discomfort with vulnerability and fear of death. It is true that discussions about death and displays of grief can cause anxiety and denial, but the grieving person is not blamed for her condition. There is no stigma attached to grief and no corresponding shame. The public toilet analogy that opened this work, illuminating the perceived exposure of the lonely, does not operate the same way for the person in mourning.

The "aura of untouchability" has to do with the perception that a lonely person is unloved and perhaps unlovable. We may internalize this perception and, consequently, feel the shame of our condition, as though loneliness is a fault, and it is ours. I suspect that anyone who has experienced loneliness can attest to this shame. We may feel it when we are alone in public, when others seem so unambiguously and happily together—on holiday weekends, for example, when we are the only ones walking alone in a park or staying at home alone while families and friends fill backyards around us. Or when we go out to eat alone, surrounded by couples.

These examples are contingent on varying circumstances and different personalities. Not every lonely person is reluctant to dine alone or stay home on holidays. It might depend on our location—whether we live in a city or rural area. Our responses may also depend on the reactions of others whose perceptions of our aloneness may matter more than our own; we become objects of pity and suddenly feel pitiful. When I arrive at a restaurant alone and ask to be seated for dinner am I given a seat at the bar due to the host's discomfort—vicarious shame, maybe—with my being the only person to dine alone in a restaurant filled with couples or groups of friends?

The "pariah aura" of the lonely is the display of human vulnerability, and the purest form of this vulnerability is the dying body, no longer in control of anything and unable to stop the inevitable. Death is absolute aloneness since it reduces us to pure singularity; the physical process, like the experience of pain, is uniquely our own. If the fear of loneliness is actually the fear of death, it could be an unconscious fear, for the most part inaccessible. But the parallels between the strange response to another's loneliness and the anxious response to discussing death or encountering another's grief suggest this might be right. We always risk the listener's fear of her own dying along with the denial of that fear when we write or speak about death and dying.

The uncanny feelings that an admission of loneliness provokes, and the stigma that arises, make us wary of encounters with the lonely person; we want to protect ourselves. This means we can discover something about the nature of loneliness by considering the defenses built against it.

STIGMA

The lonely display for us the nudity of existence. Human need and the fragility that accompanies it can make us profoundly uncomfortable. A homeless person's suffering can evoke the same response as a lonely person's: guilt, because we know that a few coins will not help this person beyond the comfort of a coffee or cigarette and perhaps also revulsion at bare deprivation on full display—a body that needs washing, a belly that needs filling, an emotional existence that needs tenderness and affection. Many of us do not want to be reminded of human need.

When we meet someone who tells us he is lonely, we may shrink from what we experience as a demand. We don't want to be responsible for this person's well-being, and we are afraid that he will drain us. Underlying this response might be the worry that the lonely will "infect" us with their condition.

There is only one way to write about the experience of loneliness that spares the reader a sense of strangeness—and it is to eliminate the I of the lonely. But I am not writing for the reader who wants to be spared.

IN THE VILLAGE

During my childhood, I lived in the kind of village Susan Pinker flew to Sardinia to find. She wondered why there were so many octogenarians among the inhabitants of this region and concluded it was because of their strong social connections; the villages of Sardinia offered the secret to a long and happy life—face-to-face contact. As the subtitle of *The Village Effect* promises, Pinker believes this contact "can make us healthier, happier and smarter." Optimal health and longevity are paramount in her account. To prove that isolation can kill us, she juxtaposes stories of individuals who meet an early demise after suffering from illness without the support of family or friends with those who battle death and disease successfully because they are not alone. In fact, Pinker claims that chronic loneliness alters the very genes in our bodies, telling her readers: "As incredible as it sounds, feeling isolated creates a 'lonely' fingerprint on every cell." This means we can inherit the loneliness gene from our parents just as we can inherit hypertension or kidney disease.[1]

    I grew up surrounded by siblings and a large extended family, an inner circle within a wider religious community of recent immigrants tightly bound together by piety and a traumatic past. I was almost never alone. I shared a bedroom with my sister. Family meals were opportunities for lively discussions with my opinionated parents and siblings. Weekly activities revolved around the church community. We knew every member of the church and everyone's family history, including which village they came from in the old country, any scandals associated with their names, and whether they were industrious or lazy, trustworthy or shifty, morally upright or unscrupulous. With equal enthusiasm we loved and supported or judged and spurned as the circumstances warranted. We took to heart the mandate "to be in the world but not of it," in the belief that worldliness interferes with godliness and with the homogeneity and self-sufficiency of the community.

I have only one memory of being lonely during my childhood, around the age of nine or ten, when I believed the other girls in my class at school did not want to play with me. I sat alone at recess and nursed my self-pity until my sister intervened. I remember feeling distinctly embarrassed because I had been wrong—they protested that they were happy to include me in their games at recess. The real issue was that games bored me. I wanted a confidante and a secret garden to explore with her. I would be loyal and devoted; I would share everything.

During my high-school years I had this kind of intimacy in abundance, for I had a dog, a boyfriend, and God. I confided equally in all three and would have been hard-pressed to say who was the best antidote to loneliness. Each had singular merits. The dog absorbed all my emotions without asking for anything but affection and material sustenance in return. The boyfriend provided a world, enhanced by our shared faith, purpose, and passion. God provided the eternal, unconditional love no human or canine friend could furnish. I had interlocutors. I was understood. I loved and was loved.

According to Pinker's observations, the fact that the inhabitants of Sardinia are never isolated from one another means they will live long, happy, and healthy lives. Since I left my village at the brink of adulthood, I may not be so fortunate. As soon as I ventured into the world my community had taught me to fear and condemn, I craved more of it. The comfort and security of community life, cultivated through an enforced conformity of behavior and thought, became suffocating; this is the inescapable, double-edged sword of security and the irresolvable contradiction of inclusion, which is always exclusion at the same time. So I left God and broke up with my boyfriend. I lost my dog to a clever thief.

Narrow as it was, my entire world—the community that contained it, the faith and love that colored its landscape, the future it prescribed—collapsed with a finality difficult to bear. It was my first significant experience of the deep pain of loneliness. It was also the first time I discovered there are worse things.

IN THE LONELINESS LABORATORY

Loneliness has been making headlines since George Monbiot declared in a 2014 *Guardian* article that ours is the age of loneliness, and it is killing us.[1] The pundits proclaim loneliness is on the rise in the Western world—it is our newest health crisis, a hazard equivalent to smoking fifteen cigarettes a day—and prescribe equally facile remedies.

Only a few decades ago scholars interested in loneliness lamented the dearth of literature on the subject. At that time, little seemed to have changed since the psychiatrist Frieda Fromm-Reichmann, one of the first to write a scholarly essay on loneliness, spoke in 1955 about the reluctance of her own profession to gain any scientific clarity on the phenomenon. She attributed this lack of interest to the painful and frightening nature of the experience of loneliness; avoidance serves as an effective defense mechanism. By the early 1980s, however, new empirical and theoretical studies on the causes and effects of loneliness appeared, inspired by Fromm-Reichmann's posthumously published essay on the severe loneliness of the mentally ill and by a handful of other early works.[2] Multidisciplinary volumes exploring the myriad forms of loneliness found across the psychosocial spectrum began to fill out the field.[3] The lonely person emerged as an object of investigation.

Much of this twentieth-century research describes loneliness as a pathological condition to be diagnosed and cured. In part, this is a function of social science method—the researcher observes the researched, and derives definitions and theories from surveys and statistical data in a process that leads from the particular to the general. The lonely person thus becomes lonely people, a social category worth studying for its negative effects on society, and loneliness becomes a symptom of social decay like divorce or crime, as we read in Letitia Anne Peplau's and Daniel Perlman's 1982 survey of the literature.[4] From marking symptoms, we slide into making predictions: the afflicted are scrutinized for certain characteristics that will predispose them to occasional bouts, or even a lifetime, of loneliness.

When I read these accounts—as someone familiar with prolonged periods of loneliness—I feel like a lab specimen. Here is an abridged portrait of the lonely person, culled from Peplau's and Perlman's summary of research from the 1960s and 1970s: shy and introverted. Not willing to take social risks. Exhibits low self-esteem and inadequate social skills. Prone to self-deprecation. Highly self-conscious with a heightened focus on the self. Asks fewer questions than non-lonely people when interacting with others. Tends to dwell on her own actions. Increasingly oversensitive to social cues; misinterprets or exaggerates the responses of others. Predisposed to loneliness because of these features. Less socially desirable as a result. Behavioral problems include adolescent truancy, depression, anxiety, alcoholism, and suicide.[5]

I am reminded of descriptions of other social pariahs in recent history—the single mother, the homosexual, the welfare recipient, the high school dropout. In every case the portrait of the pariah tells us more about the role of outcasts in the cultural psyche than about the outcasts themselves. What insights these descriptions do reveal are rarely shared for the benefit of those described, but rather for a community of fellow experts. When we name the pariah, we affirm the normalcy of those we believe legitimately belong to society.

The generic character sketch of the lonely person emerges from various social science definitions of loneliness. Peplau and Perlman note a number of approaches in circulation by the 1980s. There is a cognitive approach founded on the theory that loneliness arises because of a discrepancy between the types of relationships an individual would like to have and the kind she perceives she has. A second approach centers on intimacy, stipulating that loneliness arises because a fundamental human need for attachment is not being met. A social reinforcement approach attributes loneliness to isolation and lack of social support.[6] There are associated classifications: distinctions between emotional loneliness (the lack of intimacy) and social loneliness (the lack of a social group); between "good" loneliness (creative solitude) and "bad" loneliness (insufferable solitude); and between chronic loneliness and temporary loneliness. Underlying these theories are different understandings of the fundamental nature of loneliness—as an experience, a condition, an affective state, a feeling of lack or absence.[7]

We could argue that each of these approaches provides some truth about loneliness, but rigid classifications risk eliminating the fluidity and complexity of a range of experiences associated with loneliness. For example, the line between emotional and social loneliness becomes indistinct when we consider that both the desire for intimate love and the desire to belong are social, and both impact emotional life. What separates them is only the degree of closeness: in a coupled relationship we find the most intense intimacy and the closest physical proximity, whereas in a neighborhood we experience less attachment and a more distant proximity. We might suffer deeper emotions on parting with a lover than on moving out of a neighborhood, but the reverse may also occur—it may be a relief to leave a partner and heart-wrenching to leave a place we have called home. The human need for intimacy does not stop at the need for a lover or partner but extends to wider forms of sociality that protect us from isolation and loneliness.

The argument that loneliness is either cognitive or emotional is similarly reductive; it ignores the intertwining of the body and psyche. To believe my loneliness is due to the perception that I lack sufficient intimacy is to assume there are no objective conditions for my loneliness and that my entirely subjective perceptions are untrustworthy. We wouldn't tell a starving person they will stop craving food if they adjust their expectations for it because we perceive physiological hunger to be an objective condition with observable (and eventually fatal) effects if the desire for food is unsatisfied. If loneliness is considered an emotional state, it seems reasonable to suggest that we have some control over it; that to be released from loneliness all we have to do is adjust our expectations of others. But I would argue that loneliness is a desire, not an emotion in itself, and desires are not so easily relinquished. Even if they were, we need to ask whether we *should* let go of our desire to be close to others.

In more recent scholarly treatments of loneliness, this belief in the lonely person's control over her condition is still prevalent. For example, the editors of a 2017 volume, who promise to attend to the contemporary complexities of loneliness, write in their introduction that loneliness is a problem only when an individual "deems it to be so," which echoes Epictetus, the Stoic thinker who wrote, "it is not what happens to you, but how you react to it that matters."[8] There is certainly wisdom in the advice of this first-century Greek slave-turned-philosopher; he reminds us of our inner resources. He argues persuasively that in the face of adversity, when we cannot control our circumstances, we can still control our emotions and attitudes. "Another person will not hurt you without your cooperation," he writes, "you are hurt the moment you believe yourself to be."[9] On loneliness he might say: you are only lonely if you believe yourself to be lonely. Suspend your desire for intimacy and you will no longer suffer. But Epictetus is thinking about the situations we do not have the ability to change. If the conditions of loneliness can be changed, the pain we feel when we are lonely should not be something we accommodate. We wouldn't tell the hungry person to forget about her cravings if someone or something were preventing her from eating. And wouldn't it be similarly cruel to advise a lonely person to adjust to deprivation, to detach from his desires when what he desires is attachment?

If ours is the age of loneliness, as Monbiot has concluded, it is also the age of anxiety—accompanied by risk-aversion and a desperate desire for guarantees. The new warnings about a loneliness epidemic are shrill and sensational. Loneliness is "lethal," Judith Shulevitz warns; it will ravage your body and your brain.[10] Like Susan Pinker in *The Village Effect*, Shulevitz draws from studies that allegedly prove the lonely are more prone to such conditions as cancer, dementia, diabetes, high blood pressure, heart disease, neurodegenerative diseases, even the common cold, and compares these ill effects to the outcomes of obesity or smoking. Relying on the research of John T. Cacioppo—hailed as the founder of the field of social neuroscience—both Pinker and Shulevitz argue that loneliness is in our genes and has the power to alter DNA transcription in the cells of our immune systems.[11]

When loneliness is called a public health crisis, it is treated like any other health crisis: we name and classify an affliction and search for a cure, stigmatize a population we decide is prone to the disease, and assemble a vast network of experts who promise remedies for the afflicted and guarantee immunity for everyone else. The social causes and effects of loneliness tend to recede or, at most, appear in a conventional, conservative guise. The crisis may be attributed to modern individualism, digital technologies, the weakening of family ties, and the urban erosion of community relations, but the status quo is rarely contested. This makes for some sloppy reasoning that quickly dissolves into moralism.

Consider, for example, that despite her emphasis on the genetic basis for loneliness, Shulevitz informs us that the lonely are "the outsiders: not just the elderly, but also the poor, the bullied, the *different*." To explain, she resorts to the well-worn predictors of social pariahdom: a lack of love at the start of life, poverty, divorce, and being raised by a single mother (who doesn't have time or money to engage in "emotionally enriching social activities").[12] If family ties are weakening, it is marriage that will save us. Pinker also hails marriage as an antidote to loneliness, enumerating the psychological benefits of this unique social support system: stronger and more stable relationships, better mental health, happiness, longevity, and a decreased tendency to alcoholism or depression. When it comes to physical health, Pinker claims married people can expect "significantly" reduced chances of being hospitalized, needing surgery, dying after surgery, or developing pneumonia, rheumatoid arthritis, gum disease, a viral infection, dementia, clinical depression, a serious cardiac event, or a variety of "horrible" cancers. Marriage apparently also reduces one's chances of going to jail, being murdered, dying in a car accident, or dying by suicide.[13] A "good" marriage even offers resistance to colds and to existential self-doubt.[14] She fails to mention that marriage also kills—mostly women, to be precise.

No matter where they are on the scale of social versus psychological explanations, the current loneliness experts tend to pathologize loneliness and make the lonely responsible for dealing with their affliction—just as their twentieth-century scholarly forebears did. Cacioppo, ignoring the social altogether, believes the genetic basis of loneliness determines how vulnerable we are to social disconnection; beyond genetics, we are responsible. He insists that how we experience loneliness depends on both the capacity to regulate our emotions when faced with this social disconnection and our ability to adjust our expectations of others.[15]

This is the cheerful promise of cognitive behavior therapy. Cacioppo's approach is seductive because it empowers us: if the lonely can modify their responses to others, they can control the pain of loneliness. But on the flip side, if they are responsible for rising above their suffering, they are also responsible for failing to do so. Cacioppo does not spare the lonely person when he describes this failure. When the lonely are unable to adjust their need for attachment, he tells us, they begin to anticipate danger in any social situation and view others in more negative terms, which leads to the very rejection they fear. He gives an example of a lonely roommate at a social gathering who "throws around snide comments all evening," then complains she is being criticized when others protest. When an argument ensues, she is the one who yells, while others remain calm and reasonable. The outcome for the lonely is more distrust and more loneliness.[16]

In Cacioppo's account a downward spiral follows the failure of the lonely to modify their expectations. Their inability to self-regulate extends to all aspects of their lives, which leads to hostility, depression, despair, and impaired social skills. These, in turn, may lead the unfortunate, lonely person to seek solace in "unwise sexual encounters, too much to drink or a sticky spoon in the bottom of an empty quart of ice cream"; or worse, the lonely could become "more susceptible to the out of control behavior that often begins in bars and dance clubs."[17] He doesn't stop at the dance floor—divorce, estrangement from families, conflict with neighbors, bulimia, drug and alcohol abuse, suicide, premature aging, and early death are all in store for the lonely person who is unable to manage her need for attachment.[18] The only relief Cacioppo provides for the lonely in this tale of unrelenting misery is to reassure them that they are "no more or less" attractive or intelligent than everyone else—comic relief, surely, for the lonely reader.

We can summarize the loneliness laboratory approach in a line from Norwegian philosopher Lars Svendsen: "You are not lonely because you are alone—you are alone because you are lonely,"[19] which implies that our loneliness is due to some character flaw or irritating behavior that makes us undesirable social company. On Svendsen's list of flaws we find self-centeredness and lack of empathy, an inclination to talk too much, and the wish to identify as a victim. We may not be as baffled as he is by the "uncomfortable silence" that descends on his classrooms when he asks his students whether anyone is lonely.[20]

The panacea for loneliness offered by the loneliness experts reflects the belief that loneliness is a personal failure that demands a personal solution. Pinker advises her lonely readers to create a village of their own, building social contact into their days the way they build in exercise. Better yet, combine these regimens as Pinker does when she joins a swim team in order to get "more bang for [her] buck" than she could get swimming alone.[21] For his part, Cacioppo believes the lonely can "tone" down their fearful response (with his help) and take control of their lives, since, with a little encouragement, almost anyone can escape the prison of their distorted social perceptions and learn to "modify self-defeating interactions."[22] To this end, the lonely could learn from the non-lonely, who seem a happy lot in Cacioppo's account, known for elevating the collective mood without talking too much or, as the lonely are wont to do, "cast[ing] a pall over any gathering" with their personal baggage and annoying behavior.[23]

Who takes this work seriously and why are honest questions. It is reasonable to assume that some lonely people experience more health problems than those who have a supportive group of family members or friends. It may also be the case that some lonely people are lonely because they behave in ways that are difficult for others to accommodate — though surely difficult behavior is not exclusive to lonely people. Even if everyone were solely responsible for their own loneliness, we could object to the accounts of these experts on the simple grounds that castigating the lonely for their failures merely exacerbates the stigma against loneliness and worsens its attendant distress. But to ignore the many complex, structural causes of loneliness is to personalize a form of suffering and blame the sufferer, as we might blame the poor for their poverty, ignoring the global forces responsible for perpetuating a convenient system of economic inequality.

Blaming the lonely lets the non-lonely off the hook. There is no demand for social responsibility; no one else has to change their behavior or assume some responsibility for the lonely. Putting the onus on the lonely also increases the distance between the lonely and the non-lonely. Clear, distinguishing criteria are developed to separate them: the non-lonely can affirm their normal status by projecting all negative qualities and behaviors onto the lonely, down to the most absurd banalities like eating too much ice cream.

Conspicuously absent in these scholarly studies and public discourses on loneliness is the lonely person as subject, as the I of the narrative. These works do not appear to be written by the lonely and they are not for the lonely to read; the pain of loneliness is discussed from a clinical or scholarly distance that ends in moralistic condemnation. Loneliness is the problem of the lonely, which adds to the stigma peculiar to loneliness and to the perception that our social environments remain static. Whether we are lonely in 1980 or in 2020 seems not to matter. What matters is whether we have an inherited disposition that makes us prone to loneliness or whether we expect too much from our relationships.

It is worth asking whether the pathologization of loneliness—the classification of predispositions and symptoms and degrees of social dysfunction—is part of an elaborate defense against loneliness and the very source of its stigma. The loneliness experts protest too much.

THE PARADOX (II)

The one-way glass enclosure of the lonely provokes a craving like no other—to be seen and heard, to be known, to be a part of the world.

In Toni Morrison's unforgettable novel *Beloved*, a dead girl comes back to life, desperate to be loved by the mother who killed her to keep her safe from a life of slavery. But the love needed to satiate a ghost-girl's desire must be unlimited; abandoned once, she is not likely to tolerate anything less than an unconditional, omnipotent love that is beyond the capacity of any human. The girl becomes tyrannical in her demand for a mother's guilt-induced self-sacrifice; she terrorizes the household and steals her mother's lover with the words: "'I want you to touch me on the inside part and call me my name.'"[1] The implication is sexual, though rich with metaphorical possibilities. As the daughter literally and figuratively fattens on her mother's ministrations, her belly distending, the mother's body diminishes until the community women come to prevent the daughter's total dominion over her mother.

The lonely person feels the psychic equivalent of malnourishment, the paradox of an empty plenitude. When a body begins to starve, it draws nourishment from all available sources. It feeds on fat stores before turning to muscle for sustenance. Eventually the body fails to compensate for the deprivation. When nothing is brought into the body from the outside, it collapses.

When I am most lonely, I feel like this starving body. I turn inward to feed on my own resources until they are depleted. A sense of emptiness expands inside me like the belly of the malnourished. I drift into lassitude—my body curls back into itself.

This is when I understand Beloved's need to be called by name and touched "on the inside part" as the demand of every lonely person.

WHAT IS LONELINESS?

Loneliness is an experience that resists conceptualization, which helps to explain why philosophers, who thrive on definitions, neglect the subject. Like love, loneliness is complex, idiosyncratic, unreasonable, both extreme and ordinary, profound and superficial, colored by all the vicissitudes of human experience. This does not mean loneliness is undefinable; it means we must allow for these vicissitudes when we attempt to define it.

I define loneliness as an unfulfilled desire, a longing for the intimacy or closeness one does not have with other human beings. This desire is not the same as an emotion, though it inspires a range of feelings from sadness and self-pity to anger or despair. It is experienced as temporary, intermittent, or sometimes permanent. Loneliness is like hunger, which we wouldn't call an emotion but a craving based on need; when hungry or lonely, we want something indispensable to life. The craving of loneliness often feels as physical as hunger. We must not forget the body when we think about the meaning of loneliness.

I use the term "intimacy" with some hesitation, since we typically associate intimacy with a sexual relationship, which is only one way among many to be close to another person. When I speak of a need to be close to others, I refer to a spectrum of relations and intimacy, from the familiar and private sphere of a relation between two, or a very small group of loved ones, to a public world of neighborhoods, communities, and other social or political associations. To be close in this broader sense includes a vast range of experiential phenomena, from love and emotional attachment (more intimate) to civility and solidarity (less intimate), that lead to a sense of belonging and meaningfulness. To love is to bestow value on another, and when we value another, we want to care for her or him.[1] To be emotionally attached means we are (ideally) fully attuned to another's existence—understood and understanding, sensitive to thoughts and feelings—and interested in her or his well-being. When we belong, we have an essential place in the world—a home, a neighborhood, a community—where we feel we matter to others and can contribute to something larger than ourselves through our talents and interests. These relational elements of human existence contribute to a meaningful life.

Our need to be close to others is thus in evidence at multiple levels, from the private to the public and from the deeply intimate to the more superficially close. We need love, care, and understanding, but we also need to interact with neighbors and acquaintances as well as a wider public world in which we participate as members who matter to one another (even if we are in conflict). When this need for human togetherness is frustrated, our responses again fall within a spectrum, from boredom, depression, withdrawal, or malaise to incommunicability and even psychosis, as Frieda Fromm-Reichmann will tell us. To make matters more complicated, we do not all need the same level of intimacy with others, for a variety of psychological and circumstantial reasons. One person wants to be continually surrounded by others, another craves solitude; one person feels she has been lonely her entire life, another feels only occasional loneliness when separated from loved ones.

Fromm-Reichmann, an influential twentieth-century psychiatrist known for her work with schizophrenic patients at Chestnut Lodge, a Maryland psychiatric institution famous for its unorthodox approach to treating mental illness, begins her classic 1959 essay on loneliness by speculating on her own "strange fascination" with the subject. She attributes this fascination to her interactions with a young "catatonic" woman who slowly came out of a noncommunicative, isolated state when Fromm-Reichmann acknowledged the woman's loneliness.[2] The recognition of her patient's suffering was a recognition of "the need for contact and tenderness" that Fromm-Reichmann believes we are born with.[3] Our longing for intimacy stays with us throughout life, she writes, "and there is no human being who is not threatened by its loss."[4] The question is then, as Fromm-Reichmann puts it: "What has gone wrong in the history of the lonely ones?"—in those who suffer because their need for intimacy has not been satisfied.[5] This is a very different approach than the one that searches for qualities that predispose a person to loneliness. In Fromm-Reichmann's essay, loneliness is a manifestation of frustrated need. She cites approvingly the definition of loneliness offered by her colleague, Harry Stack Sullivan, as "the exceedingly unpleasant and driving experience connected with an inadequate discharge of the need for human intimacy."[6]

To offset the "terminological handicap" she finds in studies of loneliness, including in the field of psychiatry, Fromm-Reichmann makes a number of useful qualifications. Loneliness is "such a painful, frightening experience that people will do practically everything to avoid it," she writes, and this includes psychiatrists, who when they do mention loneliness lump it together with aloneness, isolation, compulsory solitude, and "real loneliness"—the loneliness that is incommunicable.[7] Yet these are each unique experiences, as anyone knows who isn't always lonely when alone or who has felt the peculiarity of alienation that is not quite loneliness and not quite isolation either.

Fromm-Reichmann proceeds to distinguish "real" loneliness from solitude, grief, temporary aloneness, a "culturally determined" loneliness (modern alienation), and a "constructive aloneness" (solitude, necessary for creative expression).[8] She stipulates that though these are not trivial experiences, they can still be communicated, unlike the form of loneliness she witnesses among those suffering from schizophrenia and psychosis. Real loneliness in her view is not a temporary state, but a condition in which a person even forgets she once had close relationships in her life and no longer hopes there will be relationships in her future life.[9] This kind of loneliness leads to "paralyzing hopelessness and unutterable futility"; it is incommunicable for it defies description and so terrifying that the lonely try to dissociate from any memory of it.[10] The fear and paralysis cannot be endured for long and can lead to psychotic states.[11] Fromm-Reichmann wonders whether such experiences of real loneliness, as well as other "uncanny" experiences possibly related to loneliness, like panic or a loss of reality, defy Sullivan's definition.[12] The point of her essay is to suggest that the line between real loneliness and mental illness is difficult to draw, for loneliness plays a far greater role "in the dynamics of mental disturbance" than has been acknowledged.[13]

As a desire for the intimacy one lacks, loneliness is thus experienced along a spectrum of intensity and suffering as well as need. It is not the same as aloneness or solitude since we can be alone without needing another. It is not the same as isolation, which is the physical or mental state of separation that may or may not lead to loneliness; we can be isolated without being lonely and lonely without being isolated. Loneliness may coincide with grief, depression, or anxiety, but these are also unique phenomena, separable from the desire for intimacy.

I have never experienced the severe loneliness Fromm-Reichmann features in her essay, but I am drawn to her account for its attention to the pain of loneliness even in its less intense forms not necessarily related to mental illness, and for locating the source of that pain in the lack of intimacy as it is lived, not as it is subjectively perceived, as Cacioppo and Svendsen would have it. Fromm-Reichmann accepts that human beings have a profound need for one another; we are dependent on others for self-validation, compassion, understanding, and for something I will simply call proximity—the physical nearness of other members of our species. The variability of this dependency explains why everyone has differing levels of tolerance to being alone. Most importantly, in the pages of Fromm-Reichmann's text we find what is missing in much of the scholarly and popular analyses of loneliness: the lonely person as subject.

To define loneliness as a desire for intimacy suggests that to be lonely is to lack love. I believe this is true only if we define love so broadly that it encompasses a wider gamut of interactions among human beings. To love and be loved is to experience intimacy, and this is a universal need no one could reasonably argue against. But our need for one another exceeds intimate love. We need to participate with others in the making of a shared world, and this collective engagement takes us beyond the realm of privately experienced emotions and longings. A person who is loved might still experience loneliness because he is not a part of something. Loneliness in this case is still a craving for what one lacks, but it is an expanded notion of togetherness we desire. In other words, we need a world in which to belong, and this, too, is about love.

To explain, I will rely on Hannah Arendt's concepts, "world" and "worldliness," terms she uses to evoke the political dimension of human existence. By political she means a public realm constituted by our speaking and acting together with others on human affairs that affect us all; the public realm is "the space of appearance," a space we do not all occupy (slaves or refugees, for example, are exiled from public life) or do not occupy all the time. Politics is not limited to governing structures that manage and organize society; it is a dimension of human existence that arises from the relations among a plurality of unique individuals. Arendt uses the Latin term *"inter-esse"* — literally, "between-being" — to designate this space between us. Here we create the world together, a world that exceeds the sum of all that individuals say and do, for every action is unpredictable and takes on a life of its own.[14]

There is a pronounced love of the world in all of Arendt's work. In *The Human Condition*, a work she had thought of calling *Amor Mundi*, we discover that a world is built and maintained by making durable objects, by creating and expressing ideas and art, and by cultivating the public spaces fostered by speech and collective action. "Worldliness" is the condition of this cultivation — our peculiarly human drive to fabricate objects and pursue projects that will outlive us, to establish something of permanence: a world for the next generation.

When we lose this worldliness and exist alongside others without sharing in this mutual project of world-building, the consequence, according to Arendt, is a devastating loneliness that "threatens to ravage the world as we know it."[15] She believed twentieth-century totalitarianism — both Stalin's and Hitler's versions — caused this loneliness through a fear-induced isolation that prevented solidarity of any kind.

Arendt's description of loneliness shares with Fromm-Reichmann's an emphasis on privation. The lonely person feels "deserted by all human companionship," which means that the self is no longer affirmed. But in Arendt's account, more than an intimate, compassionate other (or several others) is missing. Loneliness means one is "uprooted" and "superfluous"; one no longer belongs to the world, and this, for Arendt, "is among the most radical and desperate experiences" of humankind.[16]

Though Arendt had a narrow, somewhat negative, view of the social as it developed through the mass consumerism and conformity of the twentieth century, I want to make space for the social dimension of human existence in her understanding of "world." The worlds we create and belong to are as social as they are political, for these realms of human togetherness run into each other and come apart. Without the pull of friendship and common feeling there is no political engagement with the events and dilemmas that affect us all, no public debate or collective action. That the world can be ravaged by loneliness and isolation confirms social life is fundamental to human survival. Now that it is under threat — in as much danger of dissipating as our political existence—we can define the concept of world as more than a site for public discussion and action; it is a space between us, governed by an infinite variety of encounters, from mundane interactions with strangers to the intimate exchanges of friendship and love. This means we must also draw the psyche into the equation. To speak of loneliness is to acknowledge the complicated intertwining of the psychological, social, and political dimensions of life.

Fromm-Reichmann and Arendt appear to address widely different aspects of loneliness, but the desire and the suffering are the same in both accounts. In my understanding of loneliness, inner and outer, private and public, worlds must be taken into consideration. We are wholly dependent on one another, for better or for worse, and when we do not belong to a world of others, we suffer. But such dependency makes us acutely vulnerable, which can lead to a different kind of suffering. This, too, is not without its ambiguity.

THE HAPPINESS OF OTHERS

In 2010 I found myself alone in Berlin, living in a spartan studio after fleeing a destructive relationship. The loneliness that descends at the end of intimate love is particularly intense, an assault of deprivation after sensuous and emotional plenitude. My new loneliness reverberated across the empty space between the bed, the table, and the wardrobe. Through windows overlooking a courtyard, I faced seven floors of apartments on the other side and witnessed there the private lives of strangers, uncurtained until nightfall. My view: the happiness of others. As they stood over steaming pots in kitchens or aired bedding over window sills, my loneliness invented their stories. I willed them to be living in the happiness of love as much as I envied them for it.

Every morning I left my apartment in Kreuzberg for Blinis Espressolounge to write in small print on sticky notes I later taped into a notebook. Perhaps the ritual was an attempt to minimize the monumental feelings and contain them within perfectly square borders. I could order a coffee in German, but a more complicated conversation was beyond my limits; this added a unique intonation to my loneliness. I lived in a bubble, alone in a foreign country where I didn't speak the language. It wasn't fear that sealed me in, exactly, since I trusted that a kind stranger would help in an emergency. But a lot of living happens between the uneventful and the emergency. The bubble was invisible, yet impenetrable; it moved with me through the city and kept me separate. I felt more alone than I had ever felt, and this tells me something about the particular experience of loneliness when we are also grieving. There in that foreign place I was not only alone and not only grieving, but also estranged from the world. If no one speaks my language—literally or figuratively—I am wholly separate, which means I cannot escape myself. I went through the motions of living mechanically in this bubble, inducted into a new mode of anticipation: waiting for nightfall and the oblivion of sleep.

THE ALIENATION OF GREGOR SAMSA

Gregor Samsa is Kafka's travelling salesman in *The Metamorphosis*, who wakes up one morning as a giant insect. His alienation is instant and absolute. At first he thinks he will just go back to sleep and forget about the "nonsense" of his transformation, but all attempts to return to his habitual sleep position are prevented by the hard shell that now covers his body and the repulsive sight of his "wriggling legs."[1] He tries to speak to his sister, his mother and father, but the squeaks he emits instead of words are naturally incomprehensible to them. He doesn't at first understand why he is no longer interested in eating what he previously loved to eat or how to move his body by setting in motion his multiplied legs. In one poignant scene, a melancholic Gregor listens to his sister playing the violin, the music a route to "the unknown sustenance he longed for": to be close to her, loved rather than despised.[2] The reader is privy to his very human thoughts, from incomprehension to despair to the wish for oblivion. He is doubled—a human consciousness and an insect body—perfectly estranged from everything familiar and loved, including his own self.

Loneliness and alienation are close experiential cousins. I have defined loneliness as craving some level of intimacy that one lacks, a drive or desire that arises out of specific conditions that vary among persons and situations. Alienation is one of these conditions, a state of being that is characterized by feelings of separation or detachment. We feel like aliens in unfamiliar territory; we do not belong. We do not need to live in a foreign country to experience the alienation produced by a language barrier. Alienation is not the same as loneliness or isolation, though they overlap. I am alienated when I feel I don't belong. I am a foreigner, a stranger; I am not understood. If loneliness signals the lack of intimacy with others, alienation signals the lack of familiarity, of being at home with others in a world of our making.

Estrangement is a common synonym, equally evocative. When we are among strangers in a foreign country, we feel exactly as we might when living with a loved one who has become estranged from us. We begin to exist as if we were strangers in our own homes, no longer recognized or understood. Alienation may not be the result of disliking an intimate partner but about an emotional and psychological detachment that ultimately makes us feel detached from ourselves; this is what makes alienation intolerable. We dread going home, feeling a distress perhaps as physical as it is psychological when we occupy the same room, two bodies that give each other a wide berth, a sea of incomprehension between them.

We know we are strangers to ourselves when home ceases to be home, because home is by definition the place where we are most ourselves. We should not need to perform for others at home. We are in an environment of complete intimacy and familiarity; daily existence is oriented around the things we own and cherish, and around the life of anyone who shares our home. When a foreign space has expanded between two occupants, home itself becomes a foreign territory. We no longer speak the native language or understand the customs.

The thinking person, the "zealot of seriousness" as Susan Sontag called herself—always wary of the fickle currents of public sentiment, always on guard against dogma and ideology, always ready to engage in critique—is susceptible to alienation in a society that promotes the achievement of maximum happiness by the shortest route. So is the creative person in a technocratic culture, the sensitive person among unfeeling people, the recent immigrant in a small town, and so on. Alienation blurs into loneliness; the distinction between them is not always easy to clarify. But they have different settings: I can be lonely whether I am in a crowd or alone, but I am only alienated when among others. To feel like a foreigner, we need to be among others with whom we had hoped to feel at home.

THE PHILOSOPHER STANDS ALONE

Few philosophers have reflected on loneliness and fewer still have analyzed it in depth, but when they do broach the subject, they tend to conflate loneliness with aloneness. This introduces a different element into my discussion: loneliness defined as the individual's fundamental separateness—not as the desire for intimacy or a pathological state but as a condition of human existence. From this point of view, though we spend our lives among others, we are existentially alone.

The claim that we are separate in an absolute sense, bounded by an individual body or singular mind, is proclaimed by writers and philosophers alike, who echo the character Val in Tennessee Williams's play *Orpheus Descending*, when he says, "We're all of us sentenced to solitary confinement inside our own skins, for life."[1] Octavio Paz, for example, opens *The Labyrinth of Solitude* with a reference to the revelation of aloneness that he believes comes to us in adolescence, a self-discovery that opens "an impalpable, transparent wall—that of our consciousness—between the world and ourselves."[2] "We are born alone and we die alone," he writes, and this aloneness (Paz calls it "solitude") is the most profound fact of the human condition. Paz believes that feelings of loss and abandonment result from being expelled from the uterine home; loneliness is "a nostalgic longing for the body from which we were cast out."[3]

For Virginia Woolf our aloneness is constituted by the unknowable between us. Paz's "impalpable wall" of separation becomes a "virgin forest" or "snowfield" where "we go alone, and like it better so," for "always to have sympathy, always to be accompanied, always to be understood would be intolerable."[4] She protests it is an illusion to think the human world is "so tied together by common needs and fears that a twitch at one wrist jerks another."[5] Aloneness for Woolf has to do with our inability to fully know the souls of others, or our own, for that matter; the virgin forest is a metaphor for this unknowability. There is no melancholic lament here, no expression of the suffering of loneliness; Woolf is giving us a brief ode to the fundamental separation between one self and other selves. The affirmation of our fundamental separateness is at the same time a desire for the solitude required to maintain it.

Clark Moustakas provides in abundance the melancholy that Woolf lacks, yet seeks to turn the "terror" of existential loneliness into a joyous solitude. He describes his experience of being "a solitary, isolated, lonely individual" as "painful, exhilarating, and beautiful." The exhilaration has to do with the awareness of the self, which Moustakas believes inspires new sensitivities toward oneself and others. It is only when we are alone that we develop our inner resources and become "deeply in touch with [our] own existence." He concludes that it is courageous to accept existential loneliness and "a sickness" to fear it.[6] Aloneness makes us strong.

There is an element of the divine in Moustakas's narrative of loneliness, as there is for the philosopher-theologian Paul Tillich. Loneliness is a spiritual experience for Moustakas, evidenced in his many examples of individuals, from Saint-Exupèry to Emily Dickinson, who claim a monastic or ascetic space of solitude in order to deepen a sense of self and meaningfulness. Tillich claims that aloneness is overcome not by opening oneself to the world but by opening to the divine. Death is again held out as proof of our fundamental aloneness, since we are alone as we anticipate death, and no amount of communicating this anticipation to others can eliminate the loneliness of this fact. Even if we die in the presence of others, "it is our death, and our death alone, that we die"—and "who can stand this loneliness?"[7] Compounding the loneliness of death is the aloneness of the individual will that moves toward it; for Tillich, we are solely responsible for what we have done, which means that guilt cannot be shared, it is ours alone. We are fated to be alone. Even sexual intimacy fails to overcome our separateness, because the union of bodies is followed by the shame of having "given too much of ourselves," which exacerbates our isolation "even to the point of repulsion."[8] Tillich believes the only way to turn the pain of this loneliness into joy is through union with the divine; there is no repulsion in this intimacy. When we embrace aloneness our inner self is elevated to the divine, and through God we can meet other lonely selves. It follows, for Tillich, that "in one hour of solitude we may be nearer to those we love than in many hours of communication."[9]

These writings are hardly representative of the body of work that insists on our fundamental aloneness, but they do give us an indication of how we might perceive the separate nature of the self as a condition intolerable to varying degrees, yet beneficial—a strength or virtue, a necessary, insurmountable border between individuals. From this perspective, human togetherness—in the social world or even between lovers—can pose a threat to the self. One can give too much of the self and risk sacrificing self-development or self-awareness; one can even be understood too much. It is worth pointing out that when the body is removed from the equation, intimacy is suddenly safe; there is no price to be paid when one is intimate with a spiritual entity. A god can assuage loneliness without exchanging it for the risk of vulnerability.

A belief in the fundamental aloneness of human existence leads to a number of perspectives that sometimes appear in conjunction. We find an emphasis on the anxiety or despair caused by our being "terribly, utterly alone,"[10] a condition that is considered intolerable yet inescapable, one we must face if we are to live truthfully or authentically. We also find a celebration of our fundamental aloneness as the basis for autonomy; in this view we must embrace our aloneness to escape the confines and conformism of society, which pose a perpetual threat to the independent self. In these perspectives, hubris appears: I am alone, the solitary philosopher declares, *I need no one*. To be separated from others by an impassable gulf or impenetrable wall becomes a virtue, and vulnerability to others, a curse.

If it were simply a matter of acknowledging the separate nature of the self, there would be little with which to disagree. We experience ourselves as unique; every human being is a self, and each self is alone in the sense of its singularity. Consider the body. It is true that a uniquely individual body comes to be at birth and ends in the moment of death. In between the beginning and the end our embodied experiences are individual, subjective, even when they are shared among a group and become objective. An itch or tickle that I feel on my skin, to use Edith Stein's example, is a subjective feeling, and even if the feather tickling me tickles another, we nevertheless experience the sensation uniquely as separate individuals.[11] Through empathy we can identify with another body's sensuous experiences—with pain, for example—but this sensation is not experienced on our own bodies. The other's pain is experienced by "standing in the other's place."[12] But we can never live in the other's body; my separateness is always confirmed by the boundaries of my own body.

If the body is separate in an absolute sense, so is the individual will, which is responsible for motivating each of us to act. We create our singular life stories through our individual choices and acts, within the context of the unique circumstances into which we are born. While these stories are made in relation to a world of others, we alone are responsible for how we conduct our lives, albeit within the limits of our circumstances. On this point, I draw on the philosophical and literary tradition of existentialism, which values the separateness of an individual life that is inherently and absolutely free, and engaged in continually recreating the world through choices made and actions carried out. Responsibility accompanies the agony of freedom—the agony is due to this responsibility. We can blame no one for what we have done, even when actions are carried out with others. Furthermore, our choices and actions have a collective effect. We are responsible not only for our own life narratives but also for the character of the world we are continually redefining with others. There is always a personal choice to be made, no matter the circumstances. If we alone are responsible for our actions, we are also alone in our guilt.

But there is more to the insistence that we are existentially alone than an acknowledgment of the separate nature of the self due to the uniqueness of a body, will, or conscience. The self can loom large in this insistence, not merely separate and unique but invulnerable and masterful. Jean-Paul Sartre's understanding of responsibility, for example, is perhaps more absolute than it needs to be. "We are alone, with no excuses," he argues;[13] we cannot blame our bad decisions and wrongful actions on the facts of our birth, our present circumstances, or on those with whom we acted. To assign blame is always a temptation, given the unbearable nature of individual freedom. There is no God to justify our actions either—at least according to the atheist proponents of existentialism, Sartre included. In this aloneness human beings exist only to the extent that they fulfill themselves as plans or projects. We are nothing more than "the ensemble of [our] acts," Sartre writes, nothing more than our own individual lives.[14] If I go to war, I have chosen it, it is my war, he famously claims, for I could escape it by desertion or suicide.[15]

I am always surprised by the eagerness with which students embrace these ideas when I teach existentialism. They are perhaps enamored by an omnipotent will and absolute freedom, believing Sartre tells us we can do whatever we want, and no amount of complicating the narrative loosens their grip on this idea. We are used to the unlimited choices of the consumer within a culture marked by fierce individualism and weakening community ties. It doesn't help that Sartre is not entirely persuasive in his defense of existentialism when faced with public criticism of its individualistic perspective. To support existentialism's emphasis on human relatedness, he claims that though we begin with Descartes's formula "I think, therefore I am," we must also have contact with others to acquire truth about ourselves. As Sartre puts it, "The other is indispensable to my own existence, as well as to my knowledge about myself."[16] However, the "I" does not seem to be displaced from its sovereign centrality here; we might well ask where the "we" is in this claim.

The aloneness of being human, of bearing up under an absolute responsibility and accepting an anxiety-inducing freedom, is so pronounced in Sartre's work that the self-made individual begins to look like a caricature inflated with self-assurance and mastery. Consider Antoine Roquentin, the protagonist of Sartre's novel *Nausea*, a kind of existentialist prototype, who is always alone with his dreary reflections on life, bored, alienated, and sick over the random, purposeless nature of existence. Even in Sartre's ideas on love we find estrangement, for he believes love is a conflict. Love begins with an "enterprise," a project of the self, to procure the love of another by making oneself "a *fascinating object*."[17] In order for the enterprise to succeed, says Sartre, "I must no longer be seen on the ground of the world as a 'this' among other 'thises,' but the world must be revealed in terms of me." When loved, "I am the world."[18] Finally, we must not forget Garcin's famous line in *No Exit*, Sartre's play about three disagreeable people who discover with horror that they have died and are confined together in a room for eternity: "Hell is—other people."[19]

The unrelieved aloneness of Roquentin is mirrored in Albert Camus's choice of Sisyphus as his existentialist hero. Sisyphus is a character from Greek mythology, a man condemned to push a rock up a mountain for eternity as punishment for repeatedly deceiving and defying the gods. In the original myth Sisyphus is a trickster—deceptive and conniving—but Camus pays little attention to this; he is preoccupied with Sisyphus's scorn. "There is no fate that cannot be surmounted by scorn," he writes, describing Sisyphus as "the master of his days" and "superior to his fate" because of this defiance of the gods.[20] Camus imagines Sisyphus happy despite the futility of his eternal task, especially in those moments of respite when he returns to the foot of the mountain after the rock has rolled back to the bottom. The significance of this "pause" is ignored in artistic renditions of the myth; Sisyphus is often depicted heaving his rock up the incline with exaggerated masculine features, an obscenely muscled body shouldering its burden against the backdrop of a bleak landscape, defiance in every detail.[21] The irony is that Sisyphus's defiance and scorn are incapable of altering his fate. What meaning can his "absolute" freedom have if he is forced to obey the gods forever? Sisyphus is free to think what he wants, and this is not nothing, but it is a limited freedom without worldly meaning. It is also a lonely freedom, one that bears little relation to the freedom Camus has in mind when nearly a decade later he writes *The Rebel*, amending Descartes's "I think, therefore I am" to "I rebel—therefore we exist."[22] The "we" would have made a difference to Sisyphus, both in life—it may have tempered his deceptiveness—and in the afterlife—teamwork would have lessened his burden.

The emphasis on mastery is ironic in light of the staggering destruction that formed the historical context of French existentialism, an irony noted by Simone de Beauvoir in *The Ethics of Ambiguity*, published in the immediate aftermath of the Second World War. In the marvelous opening passages, she describes the excruciating paradox of human existence, for human beings are the "supreme end" of all actions and events, yet subject to the contingencies of history and compelled to treat others as means. And so

> the more widespread their mastery of the world, the more they find themselves crushed by uncontrollable forces. Though they are masters of the atomic bomb, yet it is created only to destroy them. Each one has the incomparable taste in his mouth of his own life, and yet each feels himself more insignificant than an insect within the immense collectivity whose limits are one with the earth's.[23]

THE PHILOSOPHER STANDS ALONE

In this passage de Beauvoir exposes the hubris of the fantasy for autonomy and mastery. Like Sartre and Camus, she stresses that the individual is a "sovereign and unique subject" in a world of objects, but she recognizes the dependency of the individual on others rather more than they do. Philosophers have always tried to "mask" what she calls the "tragic ambiguity" of the human condition—the individual is sovereign at the same time she is impotent in the face of crushing forces. We might ask whether the mastery is a myth to begin with if "uncontrollable forces" might crush us at any moment. We "taste" our own life as utterly unique and sovereign subjects, and yet we feel as insignificant as insects against the backdrop of an unpredictable, uncertain world crowded with others on whom we necessarily depend. Individual sovereignty is an illusion.

The insistence that human beings are alone and must embrace this aloneness begins to sound like a defense against it. Perhaps it shouldn't surprise us that existentialism became popular in the aftermath of a war in which millions of people died. Declarations of "I am alone" or "I am the world" might constitute a reasonable defense against random destruction and death. The feeling of insignificance that is the mark of existential anxiety might matter more in these declarations than the absolute aloneness and sovereignty of the individual, or at the very least the insignificance and the sovereignty are deeply imbricated. I feel insignificant when facing a mountain range, witnessing a storm over an ocean, looking down from a great height on a city street full of milling crowds, or thinking about the earth's four-and-a-half-billion-year history. Suddenly I experience what is central to my own life—interests, desires, emotions, obsessions, accomplishments, and failures—as unimportant as dust motes. This must be the experience of victims of natural disasters or war, as de Beauvoir implies. With the insignificance may come the feeling that nothing matters, and that our lives are completely out of our control. We fail to overcome our circumstances because we are not free to do so. Events are random. We are mortal and our mortality, as well as the sheer number of others who share it, reveal the indifference of the universe. Camus famously calls this predicament "absurdity," which simply refers to the intolerable contradiction in the fact that there is no absolute meaning or purpose in life, yet we perpetually strive to find it anyway.[24]

There is no discussion of loneliness in these existentialist preoccupations and no yearning for closeness to others. There is certainly suffering—due to alienation, the agony of freedom, and the aloneness of responsibility—but this suffering is believed to make an individual stronger. We can trace the origins of this claim back to French existentialism's precursor Nietzsche, who coined the phrase "Whatever does not kill me makes me stronger."[25] Anyone who knows something of Nietzsche's life will see the irony in this line; he was tormented by loneliness and mental and physical illness. Lou Salomé, who knew Nietzsche and his loneliness personally, believed his inner life and work must be understood through his loneliness and suffering, "the two great lines of fate in Nietzsche's biography."[26] Salomé's descriptions of the sensuous expression of his loneliness are poignant: "In a dark mood," she writes, "his loneliness would speak gloomily, and almost threateningly, from his eyes as from uncanny depths, depths in which he always remained alone and which he could share with no one. At times, these depths gripped him with horror, and in these his mind finally drowned."[27] The inextricable relation between mental illness and severe loneliness that fascinated Frieda Fromm-Reichmann is no doubt in evidence here. Yet everywhere in Nietzsche's work we find loneliness concealed through a celebration of self-governing autonomy, of the man who commands himself.

It seems reasonable to conclude that this valuation of autonomy defends us against the pain of loneliness. We could read the omnipotent will and scorn of the self-made man as a defensive strategy to ward off vulnerability, to repress dependency on others in order to guard against the "rabble" as Nietzsche would put it, and to counteract "the need for excessive internal and external closeness to loved people," as Melanie Klein suggests.[28] This is no longer merely an acknowledgment of the separateness of the self but an affirmation of the necessity of this separateness. To be alone is a virtue, a sign of greatness, and to recognize and accept this aloneness is to develop an autonomous—even genius—self.

We find the American version of this genius springing out of splendid aloneness in Ralph Waldo Emerson's famous 1841 essay, "Self-Reliance." "We must go alone," he directs his fellow men, for we have to trust only ourselves—not the ideas and traditions from the past—as do the men of genius who believe what is true for them is true for all men. Society is a threat in this essay, conspiring against "manhood," demanding that we surrender self-reliance. It is not only the crowd but those closest to us that we must avoid—even fathers and mothers, wives and brothers must be shunned when genius calls. Emerson criticizes any focus on the commonality of others; society is referred to as a "crowd" or a "mob" in a derogatory sense. Acts of hospitality and affection are lies; the silent church before a preacher begins preaching is preferable; travelling is even unsound. Emerson complains that men have become timid and apologetic, no longer "upright" because they quote sages and do not dare to say "I think"—they merely imitate. But the great man (presumably Emerson himself) knows there are no "footprints" of others in his thought. Even institutions are only the "lengthened shadow of one man."[29] The I is omnipotent.

The genius Emerson describes would not rely on others, for this would be evidence of sheer weakness. He would refuse to mimic others' ideas and would keep "with perfect sweetness" his independence and solitude in the midst of others. It follows that no one should be allowed to rely on the great man either. "I must be myself," he insists, for "I cannot break myself any longer for you, or you." There is no room for a "we" in this glorious self-reliance. Emerson asks rhetorically, "Is not a man better than a town?"[30] Society itself is "barbarous," never advancing yet always changing. There is no social life in this account, no space of appearance or worldliness. For Emerson, the self, in union with the divine, has absorbed everything into itself.

After assembling this narrative on human aloneness that doubles as a defense against it—a call for a self-made man, master of his own life, defiant against God or the world (or conversely, claiming unity with God)—I search for relief in *A Room of One's Own*. Here we find Virginia Woolf's narrator speculating on the reasons for her century's "stridently sex-conscious" writings, to which so many books about women by men attest, and concluding that the suffragist movement had both challenged men to think about their own sex and roused in them "an extraordinary desire for self-assertion." Opening a novel by "Mr. A," Woolf's narrator admires his confident writing—the product of an excellent education and the benefits of freedom since birth. But then she notices a shadow that extends across the page, a "straight dark bar" shaped like the letter "I" that a reader tries "dodging this way and that" to see what lies behind it. "One began to be tired of 'I,'" Woolf writes, not but what this "I" was a most respectable "I"; honest and logical; as hard as a nut, and polished for centuries by good teaching and good feeding. . . . But—"I am bored!" But why was I bored? Partly because of the dominance of the letter "I" and the aridity, which, like the giant beech tree, it casts within its shade. Nothing will grow there.[31]

We need to protect the separateness of the self, for in this solitary, private space the life of the mind is nurtured, and the energy of an individual will is stimulated. But the question is whether we need to do so at the expense of the we. The I does not have to create a desert in its shadow.

IN THE HOLE

For the prisoner in solitary confinement there is no escape from the shackles of the self; isolation and loneliness are one. Cell walls are like the walls of the self, letting nothing in, but nothing out either. There is no exchange, no shared world in which one's opinions and actions matter, nothing to make a person worthy of life. There is only intense boredom and the living death of sensory and social deprivation.

There is nothing to confirm the existence of the prisoner in the hole; imprisoned within a self, deprived of any mental and sensuous movement beyond the self, he passes through stages of anxiety, hyperactivity, then depression, and extreme passivity.[1] His brain deteriorates, often beginning a mad descent into violence and psychosis. The loneliness of solitary confinement might be experienced as the worst form of torture.

A CIA counterintelligence manual from 1963, explaining the methods and rationale for the interrogation of prisoners, cites researchers who list "an intense love of any other living thing" as one of the typical effects of solitary confinement.[2] The need to escape from the self into companionship and conversation is like the "gnawing appetite" of a starving person, the researchers conclude.[3]

Even insects provide a mode of escape. Terry Anderson, the American diplomat who was held hostage by Hezbollah in Lebanon from 1985 to 1991, tells how he craved not only companionship but activity as he passed interminable hours observing the roaches crawling across his cell walls.[4]

The stress caused by social isolation and sensory deprivation damages the hippocampus region of the brain, sometimes permanently, and causes, among other changes, impaired memory and loss of the ability to navigate—even the terrain of faces.[5] After twenty-nine years in a six-by-nine-foot prison cell for all but one hour of every day, Robert King was for a time after his release incapable of recognizing faces.

Anthony Graves spent more than eighteen years on death row in Texas and testified that he had "no physical contact with another human being" for at least ten of those years. After his release, he had trouble being with others for long periods of time without feeling "crowded."[6] The sensory overload of the sight, sound, and touch of another body after extreme deprivation would be unnerving if not suffocating.

The sensuous body adapts for a time to its malnutrition. Jack Henry Abbott, who estimates he spent about fourteen or fifteen years in the hole of US maximum-security prisons, describes his dulled senses—his ability to discern only a few drab colors and feel only concrete and steel. Relating his experience after release, he says, "I could not orient myself. The dull prison-blue shirts struck me, dazzled me with a beauty they never had. All colors dazzled me. A piece of wood fascinated me by its feel, its texture. The movements of things, the many prisoners walking about, and their multitude of voices—all going in different directions—bewildered me."[7]

Without touch, conversation, mental and physical stimulation—without others—we are cut off from experience itself. The deprivation of any exchange with a living planet and its inhabitants, the reduction of experience to an encounter with the self only, is death, Abbot tells us. "When life ends, the living thing ceases to experience. . . . So when a man is taken farther and farther away from experience, he is being taken to his death."[8]

I think of Abbot dazzled by colors and confused by others moving around him, and of King's failure to recognize the face of someone he knows, when I consider the dystopian possibility that all our future social relations will be mediated by technological devices, dulling our senses and prohibiting experience—perhaps irrevocably.

THE AMBIVALENCE OF SOLITUDE

In 2013, the elusive thief who had survived nearly three decades alone in the woods of Maine by stealing provisions from area cabins was finally caught. The story of Christopher Knight's reclusive life has sparked more than a little excitement since his capture. At the age of twenty, after quitting his job near Boston, Knight took a road trip to Florida and then headed back north, passing his childhood home in Maine, until he reached a spot remote enough to satisfy his desire to live in total isolation. There he abandoned his car and, with not much more than a tent in his possession, started walking, eventually setting up permanent camp in an enclave of rocks in the North Pond region of Maine. To survive, he stole food, batteries, propane, tools, and anything else he needed from summer cabins in the area until he was finally caught after twenty-seven years and some thousand break-ins.[1]

The public fascination with the story is as interesting as the story itself. The figure of the hermit who wanders off into the wilderness, renouncing the world and its temptations, promises freedom from the pain of human interaction and from the vulnerability to others responsible for this pain. A reclusive life conjures a sage freed from the noise and speed of the world with its inevitable human conflict, greed, and violence, whose unrelenting solitude leads to self-understanding and insight into the meaning of life.[2] Michael Finkel, the only journalist Knight agreed to speak to after his capture, admitted to feeling "like some great mystic was about to reveal the Meaning of Life," yet when he pressed Knight to share his insight into the human condition, the North Pond Hermit's only advice to the world was to "get enough sleep."[3]

There was no reason for his retreat into the woods, he admitted, other than to be alone; he had no plans and "wasn't thinking of anything."[4] Following a similar search for hermit wisdom, Paul Willis writes of his dashed expectations when the "minor-league Thoreau" he hoped to find in an abandoned silver mine in Arizona turned out to be a volatile drunk who hated everyone and everything.[5]

Our search for insights on life from those most detached from it—at least from all but the most interior life—may be the result of a long history of religious figures who sought enlightenment in seclusion and a philosophical tradition enamored with contemplation. But solitude in these histories is not always as pure as it appears. In a BBC discussion with Simon Blackburn and Melissa Lane on the philosophy of solitude, John Haldane makes a case for reading the history of Judeo-Christian and Western philosophical traditions as an ambivalent movement between being alone and being with others or between separation and attachment. We find recluses living centuries before the birth of Jesus for whom the desert was the chosen wilderness, a place of escape as well as purgation, where life was "pared down to the bone" as Haldane puts it. In the ninth century BCE the Hebrew prophet Elijah is referred to in the Qur'an as the "prophet of the desert"; centuries later John the Baptist retreats into the desert, surviving on locusts and honey; and Jesus of Nazareth famously disappears into the desert for forty days and forty nights to wrestle with the temptations of Satan.[6]

Meanwhile, Ancient Greek philosophers elevated contemplation as the way to the best life, since they believed it is only when we stop our incessant activity that mere mortals can glimpse the eternal truth and beauty of the cosmos. Aristotle organized political life around the facilitation of contemplation; the philosopher must be freed from all the cares of daily life in order to pursue thoughts of the eternal.[7] For Plato, even love must turn away from the body toward immortality.[8]

It may be our fascination with absolute aloneness that fabricates a pure experience of solitude out of something more ambiguous. The Desert Fathers of the third century, responsible for starting the Christian monastic tradition, began as hermits and ascetics in the Egyptian desert who banded together in small groups to overcome the difficulties of surviving alone in the wilderness. Haldane points out the irony: what emerges out of the monastic tradition as a whole is community life, or shared solitude; recluses wanted to remove themselves from the temptations of society but not from others who shared their way of life.⁹ Solitude is ambiguous even in the example of the anchoresses and anchorites of the medieval era. These recluses spent their lives in prayer and meditation permanently sealed into small cells built along church walls with only narrow windows to the outside world from which they could observe mass, communicate with visitors, receive food, and get rid of waste. We learn from the *Ancrene Wisse*, a thirteenth-century book of rules for an anchoress, that she must become "utterly dead to the world" in order to facilitate spiritual intimacy with God.¹⁰ Yet our most well-known example, Julian of Norwich gave spiritual advice to visitors and published her visions in what has become one of the most important medieval texts on religious experience: *Revelations of Divine Love*. It seems hardly accurate to say Julian of Norwich was dead to the world.

An ambivalence toward solitude can be traced further in the philosophers of our Western philosophical history. Augustine of Hippo believed we could recognize God inside us only when turned away from the world, yet soon after his conversion he established a community of believers. In the sixteenth century, Montaigne retired from public life to his country estate seeking solitude in his own library to "come again to himself" while crafting his famous *Essais*. "Wives, children, and goods must be had," writes this man of means, but our happiness must not depend on them; "we must reserve a backshop" of the mind where we retreat to meet our authentic selves.¹¹ Yet we also find in Montaigne's essays a beautiful tribute to his dearest friend, Étienne de la Boétie, whose untimely death crippled Montaigne with grief.

Even in the Enlightenment era, philosophers became less enamored with solitude and more interested in sociality at the same time that they showed a new interest in being alone in nature. While Hume thought solitude risked inflating one's ego, Rousseau believed that only in solitude could the self be restored to health. In the next century, Thoreau concurred with Rousseau in *Walden*, a work that related his two-year experiment in living alone on the shores of Walden Pond in Massachusetts and promoted him to one of our most universally acclaimed advocates of solitude. The gods favored him there, Thoreau insists, for he was never lonely and in fact found company "wearisome."¹² But as it happens, Thoreau was not as alone as some of his readers would like to believe—not only did he receive a steady stream of visitors and walk frequently to his mother's home for dinner parties, but Walden Pond in 1845 was hardly wilderness. A commuter train ran to Boston along one side of the pond and summer picnickers flocked to its shores in the summer months.[13]

We may still be impressed with Christopher Knight's twenty-seven years of aloneness. In all that time, he apparently encountered another human being only once, by accident—a hiker he greeted with a short "Hi," the only word Knight claims to have uttered in nearly three decades. Yet he experienced a tenuous intimacy with others when he observed his neighbors to learn their daily habits and entered their private spaces to procure his provisions. The proof of this particular intimacy, however fleeting, was that it bothered Knight's rural neighbors more than the thefts.[14]

Our fascination with a reclusive life reflects this ambivalent movement between aloneness and togetherness. Perhaps we feel anxiety over the existential aloneness of the human condition, demonstrated by a hermit who appears to need no one, at the same time that we long for respite from the burden of others. We are divided, compelled by contradictory desires for solitude and sociality. Anthony Storr explains the contradiction well: "Two opposing drives operate throughout life: the drive for companionship, love and everything else which brings us close to our fellow men; and the drive toward being independent, separate, and autonomous."[15]

Whether we respond to the life of Christopher Knight with envy or horror suggests something about how we individually negotiate these opposing drives and whether one drive has a more powerful effect on us than the other. Can we know why we long for more solitude or crave more companionship? Frieda Fromm-Reichmann suggests our varying levels of dependence on others are responsible for how well we can bear being alone, a dependency she does not pathologize. Though all human beings rely on others for self-validation and feel threatened by the loss of boundaries in the absence of this validation, our dependence on others varies, she writes, according to the vicissitudes of personal development.[16] Since it is impossible to generalize about such vicissitudes, it is difficult to discern the boundary between loneliness and solitude.[17] Some will be deeply afraid when alone in nature, Fromm-Reichmann says—"facing the infinity of the desert," for example—while for others this setting will inspire creativity.[18]

THE AMBIVALENCE OF SOLITUDE 49

We could all locate ourselves on this spectrum of dependency and speculate on the reasons for our positions. How many hours a day, or days a week (or months or years), spent in solitude would be optimum? At one extreme, I expect we would find more than a few people who rarely choose to be alone; at the other, more than a few who rarely choose to be in company with others. The vast majority of us lie somewhere between these poles—we suffer when we have too much aloneness and suffer when we have too much togetherness. Though its causes are different, the suffering is the same: when we are lonely we feel disoriented by a loss of boundaries when others do not reflect us back to ourselves, and when we feel too crowded by others we are disoriented without the time and space to reinforce our boundaries. Any number of factors—the vicissitudes Fromm-Reichmann alludes to—come into play when we consider why we stand where we do on this spectrum: we have varying needs for validation or recognition, for affection and conversation, and for silence and reflection, as well as a complicated range and combination of personality traits—we are independent, anxious, insecure, confident, shy, gregarious, and so forth. All of these characteristics are shaped by culture and place, and by the circumstances of our birth over which we have no control.

Even if we share the same balance of the need for solitude and togetherness, it could have different sensuous inflections. My friend tells me I am brave to travel alone in a foreign country, to sit among strangers in a café, or walk among them on city streets; he would find these circumstances unbearably lonely. I listen to him describe the sublime experience of silence on a solo canoe trip in a remote region of a national park and tell him he is brave, for I would find the isolation intolerable.

To understand solitude we need to account for its chameleon nature, for one person's solitude is another's isolation. I define solitude as the pleasurable experience of being alone with myself, thinking or creating. This pleasure is what prevents solitude from sliding into the isolation that produces loneliness. Solitude is chosen; it is sought as a relief from the excessive stimulation of a loud, congested world or from the feeling of being too close to others. Knight protested to Finkel that he couldn't bear eye contact after his years alone, as a face revealed "too much information," he admitted, "too much, too fast." In solitude we find relief from sensory overload. If there is a tinge of loneliness in the pleasure of solitude, it is a kinder, friendlier loneliness simply because we want to be alone—solitude can feel as necessary as intimacy.

Yet we know from extensive research on solitary confinement and sensory deprivation that being alone can lead to the most mentally destructive isolation; despair and madness rather than pleasure are its outcomes. For those who love solitude and seek to promote its benefits to a society increasingly anxious about the erosion of traditional social bonds and a loneliness crisis, solitude's dark potential is not always acknowledged. In their defense of solitude they may inadvertently reverse the prejudice of those who pathologize the lonely, and turn what they deem an excessive dependency on others and fear of aloneness into behavior that needs fixing.

This reversal appears in Sara Maitland's quirky little book *How to Be Alone*, one part defense of solitude and one part therapy for those who fear it. Maitland lives in a remote region of northern Scotland and rarely sees anyone, which is her preference. She writes, teaches an online course, waves to the farmer passing by on his quad several times a week, and greets the postal carrier. *How to Be Alone* is Maitland's response to a culture she believes prizes personal freedom and individualism yet remains terrified of solitude. Her case in point: the stigma of the single person. Those who live alone and enjoy it are charged with selfishness or social irresponsibility, she complains. Solitude is thought to be unnatural, pathological, or dangerous—its enjoyment masochistic.[19]

Solitude is none of these things, Maitland protests. As long as it is chosen, it is good for one's health (though she acknowledges we might not be able to prove this point). She echoes the defenders of solitude who came before her when she claims to be alone bestows further rewards—it intensifies our consciousness of a self, our attunement to nature, our relationship with the transcendent, our creativity, and our sense of freedom. But Maitland mirrors the very pathologizing she dislikes in her opponents when she suggests we treat the fear of being alone as a condition like any other phobia—an "anxiety disorder" with "clear diagnostic criteria." She seems oblivious to the irony of her position when she reassures those readers who can't enjoy solitude that they do not have "a pathological psychological disorder."[20] But the qualifier rings hollow as she launches into self-help-speak, recommending that we travel alone, train our children to be alone, commune with a transcendent being, spend leisure time alone, and (oddly but perhaps usefully) memorize anything from poetry to the periodic table to help us maintain sanity in times of aloneness.[21]

More recently, in response to the injunction to stay home at the start of the Covid-19 pandemic in 2020, Maitland scorns the mass panic generated by the worry that depression and madness are the inevitable result of solitude, and cheerfully reminds her readers that solitude is not the same as isolation. "I can say with authority," she writes, "that it is simply not the case that solitude is inevitably bad for your mental health."[22] The article is accompanied by an image of Maitland sitting with her dog as she gazes into a stove's dying embers, in a dwelling that looks very much how I imagine a fourteenth-century cell of an anchoress would look—dark, uncomfortable, ascetic. Maitland's solitude would be my isolation.

What Maitland fails to take into account is the variable experience of aloneness. I think we know that solitude is not the same as isolation, but the border between them is fluid. No one is arguing that solitude is *inevitably* harmful, only that in some circumstances it can be. While *How to Be Alone* is a refreshing departure from the alarmist predictions of the loneliness experts, Maitland risks becoming as reductive as those she criticizes. One position warns that our health and well-being will suffer if we are too much alone, while the other warns we will suffer if we are too much with others. One recommends spending more time with others; the other recommends spending more time alone.

Perhaps this dualism is a manifestation of a very human tendency to want to justify our individual desires and choices in the face of incomprehension or outright criticism—in this case, our desire to spend more time in the company of others or more time alone. This was my thought when reading *Solitude: A Return to the Self,* Anthony Storr's beautiful tribute to the creative individual's need for time and space alone in order to create. Storr was a twentieth-century psychiatrist with a passion for music and literature who wrote a dozen books and became a well-loved public intellectual. His obituary speaks of childhood loneliness, isolation, and the trauma of boarding school—and a resulting compassion for others in similar circumstances.[23]

Written in the late 1980s, Storr's defense of solitude contests the modern assumption that a meaningful life arises only through intimate attachments. Love and friendship contribute to a worthwhile life, he agrees, but they are not the only routes to happiness. Human beings are directed not only to the personal but to the "impersonal," by which he means we are fulfilled by the work or projects we accomplish alone, work that contributes little to the welfare of human beings more generally. In the case of the genius—here he names Kant and Nietzsche, among others—this would entail a great philosophical work; in the case of the ordinary person, the impersonal could be the work of gardening or playing the piano. In either case, Storr makes the point that "what goes on in the human being when he is by himself is as important as what happens in his interactions with other people"; if we are valued only with respect to our interpersonal relationships—as a parent, a spouse, or a neighbor, for example—we are not valued as separate individuals.[24]

Solitude is simply the setting for the meaningful process of creative work; the meaning is the result of not only the outcome of the project— what may ultimately be shared with others—but the process itself. For Storr this means that "the capacity to be alone is a valuable resource," necessary for us to know or realize ourselves and to become aware of our "deepest needs, feelings, and impulses."[25] He establishes here an inextricable relationship between creativity, which requires solitude, and the development of a unique self. The creative person seeks meaning through what he creates at the same time that he seeks to discover his self as an individual. This is an integrative process for Storr that has "little to do with other people."[26]

The question is, are we ever not in relation to others in the larger sense of a shared world? Are creativity and self-development as solitary as Storr likes to think? I appreciate his emphasis on the value of projects; by stressing only love and friendship as avenues to a meaningful life, the value of work can be neglected. But to argue that interests are "impersonal," because they are pursued in solitude and do not benefit others directly, ignores the broader public context of any human pursuit. The philosophers Storr mentions may have produced their works in solitude, but their ideas were developed in conversation with other ideas that came before them; they engaged with a world beyond their minds and writing desks. Once published, their works created new worlds of their own as others interpreted, modified, or dismissed them. Solitary passions such as gardening are no different from the creation of concepts; they, too, contribute to a world that is always-already there and provide us with nourishment, a healthy ecosystem, or beauty. Solitude is relative; as long as we inhabit this world, we can never be alone in an absolute sense. The risk in arguing that individuation and creativity occur for the most part in solitude is to celebrate the autonomy of the individual and ignore the world she inhabits. This merely repeats the gesture of the narcissistic I; I'm thinking here of Emerson, going alone, trusting no one but himself, or Nietzsche, responding with self-aggrandizement to the torment of loneliness and illness.

It is worth mentioning that Storr's own life as a writer and broadcaster—a public intellectual despite identifying as a "loner"—does not support the claim that creativity has little to do with other people. At the time of his death, *Solitude* had been printed over 100,000 times in the United States alone, and his works combined have been translated into twenty-four languages. A *Guardian* obituary relates that Storr went into psychiatry because a tutor at his college believed he would be good at it; Storr admitted "the crucial thing was that he liked me, and thought I could do it."[27] How can we say that a self develops only in solitude? I look back over my life and behind every moment of personal transformation I can pinpoint something as momentous as love or as small as a conversation. My self has developed through thousands of encounters with friends, teachers, parents, children, strangers, lovers, and the characters and ideas of all the books I have read.

There is truth in Storr's subtitle: solitude is a return to the self. When we are alone, we are alone with ourselves. Unless we are able to silence the activity of our minds, we are always thinking when we are alone, and this is the core of creativity. That thinking requires solitude will be evident to any of us who have tried to engage in a task that demands our attention while we focus our minds on something else. We simply can't think unless we are carrying out a task automatically. When we listen to a friend but permit our mind to wander, we "return" to our friend and realize we've missed a few minutes of his confidences. While cooking a new recipe, we could drift into thoughts about a project or recent event only to wonder whether we added the right spices. Thinking absorbs us; it requires that we withdraw from the world temporarily and attend fully to our thoughts.

In her description of what it means to think, Arendt calls this withdrawal the "*stop* and think." What constitutes the act of thinking in her analysis is not mere cognition—like logical calculation—it is a creative activity that requires an attitude of absentmindedness. We absent ourselves from other activities that demand our attention as we engage in a "soundless dialogue" with ourselves, a formulation she borrows from Plato.[28] It is as though we are two selves in one, mulling ideas over with our "other" self in an attempt to understand an experience, event, or our own behavior, or to simply muse aimlessly. Any creative endeavor begins with this withdrawal—a new thought process or a work of art. This is why tributes to solitude abound in our artistic, literary, and philosophical traditions. No one can think or create without retreating to an inner sanctum where ideas, images, metaphors, or melodies can proliferate nebulously before being actualized for others. When we withdraw from the world, we return to ourselves.

If we are driven by two conflicting drives, one for togetherness and the other for separation, we have to wonder why it is so difficult to acknowledge the contradiction without defending the first or the second. It is autonomy and individuation that Storr and Maitland want to defend in their treatments of solitude. In spite of Storr's recognition of our desire for togetherness, he occasionally slips into the defensiveness we find in Maitland, simplifying the position of those who need more togetherness than these authors do. I am tempted to point out a level of uneasiness with vulnerability in Storr's *Solitude*. In his discussion of solitary confinement, for example, he attributes prisoners' trauma to the experience of complete dependence on those who can cause them harm. The prisoner in solitary is at the mercy of more powerful others—vulnerable in the extreme—and this is the source of his trauma.[29] I find this revealing, since other accounts of solitary confinement focus on the trauma of not having anyone to depend on, which is essentially the reverse of Storr's explanation, though both claims are true. The first perspective emphasizes the prisoner's fear of absolute dependence, the second, his fear of absolute independence. We are back to an existential anxiety concerning our vulnerability to others, for which we compensate by glorifying the self-sufficiency of a sovereign self. We find further evidence of this anxiety when Storr reasons that it is the "element of uncertainty" in human relationships that renders them less than ideal avenues to self-fulfillment—an argument for pursuing our "impersonal" passions. To be alone, he claims, is as much a dimension of emotional maturity and mental health as forming relationships; like Maitland, Storr concludes that we need to develop the capacity to be alone if we are "to fulfill [our] highest potential."[30]

However, if I speculate that Storr's fear of human vulnerability is a basis for his defense of solitude, I am stuck in the dialectic of pathologizing. There must be a way for us to live with the contradictory pull of desires for both solitude and sociality without establishing norms that determine when either the need to be with others or the need to be alone cross the line into neurosis. We do not choose the vicissitudes that shape our desires.

I would like to walk a fine line between these defensive positions. I want to understand the nature of this longing to be alone, a desire as powerful as the longing for human company, without suggesting there is something wrong with those who do not share this desire. I will leave the advice to others, acknowledging there are individuals who love their solitude to such an extent they feel they must discipline themselves to socialize and others who love being in company so much they feel they must learn to spend more time alone.

Must we learn to be alone, and if so, why? The defenders of solitude have provided a few responses to this question. It is only when we are alone with ourselves that we can create, and this includes all kinds of activities from thinking to artistic creation to cultivating a self. But there is something deeper underlying these responses. To defend solitude is to defend the autonomy of a separate self with its singular inner life. It follows that those who write in praise of solitude are those who cherish their independence and feel constricted by collective life. This is not necessarily the same as claiming we are masters of our destinies, standing defiantly alone against fate or God; it is a recognition that independence of thought is something to be cherished and protected. Time and space are needed to cultivate an inner life.

To be attentive, to learn the habit of concentration, requires that we have time alone, says Marilynne Robinson, pointing to a "whole mass of rich, deep loveliness" in the world that we have been conditioned not to see.[31] If we ignore this realm to which only our minds have access, it is because we don't demand that kind of thinking.

SOLUS

The fierce Protestant work ethic of my parents meant that I worked as a child throughout the summer months on the family fruit farm. Most of the work was a collective effort—picking strawberries or cherries with up to 100 other workers or processing peaches with a group of recent immigrant women. But there was little opportunity for conversation and an abundance of time for daydreaming. Sometimes I worked alone in the barn, assembling the cardboard boxes used to transport peaches to stores. I invented imaginative games to alleviate the boredom of the work. The boxes were stacked on top of one another, creating tall columns. I would think of them as humans, give them names, and fabricate stories for their lives as they grew—predictable stories based on the world I knew. Two completed stacks of ten boxes would become the parents to a third, and so on. As a teenager I sometimes worked alone in orchards and vineyards, the isolation and the tedium of repetitive physical labor relieved only by an active mind. In my spare time I spent hours withdrawing into books or writing in a diary I started when I was ten. But I did not yet have a name for solitude.

Around the age of twelve, I began to chafe at sharing a room with my sister. We drew an imaginary line down the middle of the room but failed to solve the problem of how my sister would reach the door given it was securely in my territory. On the surface this looked like an ordinary case of sibling conflict; I did not yet know that I needed time alone, a need that instigated the transformation of a small storage room in the basement into a space I claimed for myself. My younger brother hammered four two-by-fours into a piece of plywood from the scrap pile in the barn to make a table for me. I painted it blue and happily wrote sentimental poems on its rough, unsteady surface.

SOLUS

I love the word "solitude"—the sound of the word and its meaning coincide. It has a lyrical sense for me, like the musical terms "sonata," "étude," or "prelude," and a stillness to it. The Latin origin of solitude is "*solus*"—to be alone. We are alone when we are isolated or separated from others, and this can cause a painful loneliness, but the aloneness of solitude is pleasurable. When we long to be alone we say we crave solitude, not isolation.

I know well the longing to be alone. If I try to articulate what constitutes this longing, the most accurate is to say that I long for silence, for respite from external stimulation—the noise of empty chatter or traffic or busywork. It makes sense that I feel this most often after negotiating the crowds at rush hour in my city, or after several days of teaching classes and attending meetings, or after visiting relatives. My limit for being with others is sensed in a feeling of irritation and of weariness with social performance—making polite conversation, keeping controversial views to myself, feigning interest, and so on. At the most fundamental level, my desire to be alone is a longing to think. I want to let my mind wander unhindered. This is a kind of homecoming for which physical aloneness is not necessarily required. If I feel at home with another person who knows me and understands me, if I feel I don't have to explain myself or perform for anyone, separation from others is not actually necessary. But even an intimate other can interfere with my solitude.

Solitude is for me an unmitigated pleasure—until it begins to feel like isolation. At what point this occurs depends on many variables. If I have too much time alone, the pleasure dissipates into the restlessness of loneliness. Too much time might be three days if I am alone in a foreign country conversing with no one, or five days if I am able to communicate virtually with a kindred spirit, or one day if I have unshared thoughts burning holes in my head. On the other hand, if I have been together with others for several days without respite—or sometimes one hour depending on who I am with—I long for the exquisite relief of an empty room. I doubt I could choose which deprivation is worse: to be alone all the time or to be together all the time—each would be its own kind of hell.

I did not always know I had a need for solitude; more specifically, that I needed to be alone with my thoughts. This was a slow discovery that occurred with the awareness of my deeply reflective nature, helped along by boyfriend possibilities who complained—*you think too much*—meaning my questions and ruminations annoyed them. I was a "zealot of seriousness," to borrow from Susan Sontag, who considered seriousness a virtue, though I only knew this much later.[1] My need to be alone was the external manifestation of my need to think everything over. Who can reflect without withdrawing from the noise and distractions of other people, without quitting a task that requires one's undivided attention? As May Sarton puts it, solitude is necessary "to mull over any encounter, and to extract its juice, its essence, to understand what has really happened to me as a consequence of it."[2]

Sarton best articulates my own ambivalence toward being alone. A prolific twentieth-century American poet and novelist who lived alone for most of her adult life, she wrote *Journal of a Solitude*, a chronicle of the year—1972—she lived in an old farmhouse in Nelson, New Hampshire. It is remarkably free of any attempt to resolve the contradiction between the competing drives Storr describes, for closeness and for separation. Sarton expresses in equal measure the pain of her isolation and the pain of distractions from it. If she has too many letters to write, she longs for stretches of time without any obligations except those to her inner world.[3] To be without time alone is to be in "purgatory," she writes, "I lose my center. I feel dispersed, scattered, in pieces."[4] At the same time, Sarton admits her solitary lifestyle feels "frightfully lonely," like drowning or being engulfed in quicksand.[5] But there is no way to resolve the contradiction: "Without the interruptions, nourishing and maddening, this life would become arid. Yet I taste it fully only when I am alone here and 'the house and I resume old conversations.'"[6]

Sarton never fails to note that the suffering of isolation is the price a writer must pay. There is communion in this isolation, however, that defies the distinction between these terms. She writes of returning alone to her house after visiting friends or giving talks, and this is a return to herself, to the bowls of daffodils on her window sill, her pet bird, or the feral cat hoping for a handout at her door. How are we to live in the absence of such intimate relationships, she asks, when "every relation challenges; every relation asks me to be something, do something, respond. Close off response and what is left? Bearing . . . enduring . . . waiting."[7]

ALONE TOGETHER

In her 2011 study of the psychosocial effects of technology, Sherry Turkle argues that connectivity is making us more disconnected than ever. She captures the central idea of *Alone Together: Why We Expect More from Technology and Less from Each Other* with an anecdote shared at a later TED talk: Turkle's daughter gets together with friends in her living room, their bodies in close proximity, their attention on individual electronic devices. Each of the girls is alone, separate from the others, yet they are in the room together.[1] Turkle's book provides an abundance of examples of being alone together, examples so familiar to us now that it seems banal to repeat them: our smartphones cut us off from one another in public spaces; we prefer virtual connections over face-to-face conversations; we expect less from each other the more we are chained to our communication devices, and so forth.[2]

I read Turkle's book while sitting in a Toronto café surrounded by people working alone on their laptops. We confirmed her argument: there we were, alone together, absorbed by individual preoccupations and oblivious to the occupants of other tables.

But the expression "alone together" epitomizes an experience that is enjoyable for me—I can be in public, surrounded by others, yet I am alone with my thoughts—and this enjoyment complicates Turkle's critique of the negative effects of technology. I am not suggesting that if our technology pleases us, we can dismiss objections to it, but we need to consider what the pleasure implies for the critique. I share Turkle's concerns about communications technologies, but there is another way to understand our alone togetherness. We live both as individuals and as members of groups, as small as two or as large as the earth's population, which means we are always alone and together at the same time in a fundamental, existential sense. One mode of existence does not precede the other—we live in an inherently ambiguous condition, always alone together or together alone. There is no need to choose either being alone or being together with others as the most necessary for existence. They are not discrete, mutually exclusive states.

There is a rich philosophical history preoccupied with the collective nature of human existence—to be means to be-with—that nevertheless retains a strong conception of the individual ego. This history contests the self-sufficient, sovereign self we find in Emerson, Thoreau, or Nietzsche; the philosopher does not always stand alone. Arendt, for example, never loses sight of the individual's singularity, yet everywhere in her work the *inter-esse* or between-being of individuals appears as necessary for the pluralism we require in order to live together in a shared world. Earlier in the twentieth century Edith Stein writes of an "urge to unify"—we are swept up by an animated life force that keeps us oriented toward others and merged into an "experiential current" of human togetherness. The experience of community serves to release us from our "natural loneliness," but we never lose our individual egos—"the ego that is this one and no other, solitary and undivided."[3]

Martin Buber similarly retains the conjunctive nature of the individual's relation to the community. He argues that collective life helps us escape from aloneness; the more massive and powerful the group, the more an individual feels he is saved from social and cosmic homelessness and from individual responsibility. But Buber is clear that human existence is not fundamentally individual or collective because each on their own is just an abstraction. We are individual only insofar as we are in relation to other individuals, and we are collective only insofar as a collective is constituted by individuals in relation to one another. The alternative to viewing human life as either individual or collective—alone or together— is thus to reflect on the "between," elegantly illustrated by Buber in his description of a spontaneous encounter between two people that elicits something unpredictable in each one. The encounter leaves a remainder, "where the souls end and the world has not yet begun."[4]

If alone together describes the human condition, we might reconsider the claim that human beings are existentially alone because they experience birth and death in absolute aloneness. It could be said that a fetus develops alone in its mother's body and then enters the world alone. We might note, however, that to develop within another's body is hardly a solitary endeavor; the biologic systems of mother

ALONE TOGETHER

and fetus are intertwined, the fetus utterly dependent on the mother. Blood, nutrients, and antibodies are shared. The original joining of two substances, egg and sperm, occurs within another's body and the two-become-one is implanted—firmly attached to the wall of the uterus, its life-source. No one can enter the world without the collaboration of a woman's uterine muscles or, barring that, an obstetrician's assistance. So how are we ever alone? Yet we know each fetus develops into an absolutely singular and irreplaceable human being, whose genes and environmental factors interact as no one else's have, or ever will, leading us to ask: How are we not alone? The ambiguity of the human condition is already perfectly defined at conception: we are alone together.

When we ask where the individual begins and the group ends, we are faced with a host of questions: Am I alone when I think? Yes, in the sense that I am engaged in a solitary activity that is going on in my own mind; no, in the sense that every thought arises in the context of other thoughts—those of my friends, of the authors I am reading—in fact, in the context of an entire history of thinking. Are we together when sexually intimate? Yes, in the sense that the borders between bodies dissolve; no, in the sense that one person may feel something the other does not. Bodies merge and then return to their separateness. But how separate are they? Sometimes, after a lifetime together, one partner in a couple dies right after the other. Surely this speaks to a profound attachment of body and mind that defies any notion of pure aloneness. Do we experience another's pain? No, because there is no communal body that senses as a unified entity. But how do we then explain sympathy pregnancies, cluster suicides, Munchausen syndrome by proxy, or an intense empathic response to a loved one's depression?

That we die alone is often upheld as incontrovertible proof we are fundamentally alone in the world. Certainly, we could argue that no one else's body undergoes our own unique death. On the other hand, we don't actually experience our own death. We experience dying—a lifelong process—but in the moment of death we no longer experience anything. It is only others who experience our death; it is an event they must deal with, not us.

Even if we are persuaded of our absolute aloneness because we believe we are each responsible for our own actions, we can temper this "absolute" by taking into account influences and circumstances. We may be alone in our responsibility, but there is always a social context to our actions; we have inclinations and predispositions that are difficult to fight, and we are susceptible to the influence of others.

Aloneness and togetherness merge and separate, modifying our understanding of each term. When Clark Moustakas writes that loneliness is a condition of human life that enables us to "deepen" our humanity, and that we are "ultimately and forever lonely," he means we are fundamentally alone. If we evade or deny the "terrible loneliness of individual existence," he continues, we prevent "one significant avenue" of self-development.[5] But we might easily substitute "togetherness" for loneliness in this passage. We are "ultimately and forever" together with others. We must recognize this togetherness—we are terribly, utterly together, and we risk self-alienation if we try to escape this existential condition.

It makes little sense, then, to make an either–or claim about aloneness or togetherness. The human condition is inherently ambiguous: as social beings we crave a place in the world where we are always in relation, where we can attach ourselves to others and feel at home. But our coming together is ambivalent; sometimes we feel too close, sometimes too far apart. Many of us struggle to balance the continual movement between autonomy and intimacy or between individuality and collectivity. If togetherness were absolute, we would pay the heavy price of giving up our freedom to think and behave differently (in some cases, to think at all). Conversely, without togetherness, we pay the price of loneliness. Together, we can become imprisoned within a group. Alone, we can become imprisoned within a self. We must walk a fine line between these points and everyone has a different sense of balance.

PART II

WHY ARE WE LONELY?

"ORGANIZED LONELINESS"

From my inquiry into the nature of loneliness, I conclude that loneliness is part of the human condition. I do not mean by this that every human being is existentially alone; I mean that we need and desire to be close to others to varying degrees—not only because we are vulnerable and need others for survival, but because we take pleasure in the proximity of other living beings who are like us—and these needs are not always met. While I am drawn to the idea that loneliness is the outcome of being exiled from our originary home, the severed umbilical cord an emblem of a permanently disrupted union, we should not ignore the social conditions of loneliness. We may spend our lives avoiding loneliness by attaching ourselves to friends, lovers, and communities, but this process occurs in the context of a particular world that supports or stymies our efforts along the way. Whether or not these attachments meet our social needs depends to a great extent on the psychological vicissitudes that influence our position on the spectrum of longing for intimacy or for aloneness. But we must also account for the social forces that structure our lives.

This is where everything becomes further complicated. While the social worlds we find ourselves in have the potential to keep loneliness at bay, they also *produce* it. Loneliness is not only an idiosyncratic, individual experience of suffering; it is the outcome of specific conditions that arise when social forces work together on a particular group of people to bring about isolation. We are lonely because the social is failing us.

Hannah Arendt gives us a provocative example of the production of loneliness in the context of twentieth-century totalitarianism, which, for her, includes both its Nazi and Stalinist variants. In the concluding chapter of *The Origins of Totalitarianism*, after she establishes terror as the essence of totalitarianism supported by ideology, Arendt identifies loneliness as the basic human experience pervading totalitarian rule. Terror can be total only when it has defeated all opposition: "it rules supreme when nobody any longer stands in its way."[1] In order for this defeat to occur, ideological thinking is required, a purely logical exercise to which everyone submits en masse and surrenders their "inner freedom," as well as their "freedom of movement."[2] When there is no more movement between individuals—a reference to the space between us necessary for pluralism—the capacity for action is disabled.

Underlying this unique historical combination of terror and ideology, we find isolation and loneliness since terror rules absolutely only when its subjects are isolated from one another. The task of a tyrannical government is therefore to produce this isolation.[3] Fear and the suspicion it generates are tried-and-true methods: neighbor is turned against neighbor, family against family, friend against friend.

But isolation is not yet loneliness. We know this because we can be alone and isolated without being lonely, and, on the other hand, we can be lonely without being isolated. A family can be isolated from other families, for example, but still enjoy a private sphere of intimacy. Arendt claims we need some isolation, a space between us that permits the individuality of thinking and experience—what Roland Barthes calls "distance." This space gives rise to the separateness necessary for pluralism—the fact that we are all distinct from one another.[4] Isolation, or distance, in this positive sense has productive capacities—the artist creates, the philosopher thinks when isolated from others—just as the space between us gives rise to the public, therefore political, expression of our differences.

The dangerous dimension of isolation is a political matter. Politics for Arendt is not merely the work of governance but the exercise of public life, constituted by the coming together of individuals to speak and act with one another on human affairs that concern them as a collective. Isolation occurs in the political realm for Arendt because it prevents solidarity and thus impedes political life; if we are isolated from one another, we can't act as there is no one to act with us. Without collective action we remain politically impotent, and this impotence can lead to "the beginning of terror." At the very least, isolation is the most "fertile ground" for terror and always its result.[5]

Arendt stipulates that loneliness, on the other hand, has to do with our social existence; it concerns human life as a whole.[6] Recall her understanding of loneliness as abandonment and uprootedness.[7] When we are lonely, we are deserted by others, but we also lose the self that others would affirm for us, and this leads to the loss of the world in which thought and experience occur.[8] What Arendt calls the "unbearable" nature of loneliness is due to this unworldliness. The isolated, lonely masses become like the refugees of the world wars, bereft of a world to which they belong and in which their opinions matter. When they lose a place in the world, they lose distinctiveness; loneliness is a desperate experience because it is contrary to the human condition of plurality, which is founded on our fundamental difference from one another.[9] We are able to communicate about what we hold in common only because we are not the same. If we were, there would be no need for even speech to help us understand one other, for we would think the same thoughts, and act and behave in the same ways. Loneliness destroys pluralism.

Arendt uses the phrase "organized loneliness" to allude to the systematization of an experience she believes is normally suffered in marginal circumstances like old age. Organized loneliness is systemic, produced by the isolation that twentieth-century totalitarian regimes cultivated with brutal efficiency through what she calls "the iron band of terror." This is terror's unique binding agent that presses individuals together so tightly any movement between them ceases, crippling collective action. The space between people—that beneficial separation necessary for the pluralistic give and take of public life— is eliminated. Paradoxically, the iron band of terror also destroys human togetherness; as it presses individuals into an undifferentiated mass, human interaction is suppressed. Furthermore, since Arendt believes we can trust our sensual experience only because we share a common sense that frees us from an individual and therefore unreliable sense data, the iron band of terror stunts the experience of the materially and sensually given world, destroying this shared common sense.[10]

Isolation and loneliness thus pave the road to totalitarian rule by preparing human beings for domination, replacing thinking with ideology, and eliminating our common sensual experience of the world. If loneliness was once relatively uncommon, as Arendt argues, it becomes under totalitarianism "an everyday experience" of the masses. Its twofold destruction—the elimination of the space between us and the elimination of human togetherness, both absolutely vital for political, social, and psychic life—leaves us in a desert world "where nobody is reliable and nothing can be relied upon."[11] The real danger is not the desert itself, since to be human, for Arendt, means to perpetually suffer desert conditions, but feeling at home in one.[12]

That Arendt concludes her most intensive work of political thought with a reference to loneliness may surprise us. This astute political thinker persuades us to recognize how essential our social relations are—not merely for personal happiness but also for a meaningful public life capable of preventing, or at least resisting, cruel abuses of power. This is what our current loneliness experts miss when they focus exclusively on loneliness as a health crisis. Though loneliness is experienced individually, it is never simply an interior experience. The lonely person, for all her inner suffering, bears witness to the failure of the social, a failure that is politically expedient. But this expediency remains hidden; the organization of loneliness—its systemic production—masks both its political usefulness and the social failure that is its outcome.

Ours is a very different sociopolitical context than the one in which Arendt warned loneliness would "ravage" the world. We must ask ourselves: What are the social forces that organize loneliness for us in these early decades of the twenty-first century? In the urban centers of the West, when public discussions of a loneliness crisis take into account the social, they focus on the development of digital technology, especially social media, and point to other social phenomena such as divorce, living alone, the dispersal of families, urban isolation, and the loss of community ties. They are right to point to these social developments, but they do not get at the underlying structures that bind these developments together and organize loneliness into something systemic. The elephant in the room is our current digitalized version of capitalism, accompanied by new forms of power that produce, in turn, new forms of isolation and fear.

It is not new to acknowledge the synergistic relationship between capitalism and technology, as well as the alienating effects of this union. Arendt joined other critics of alienation among her generation, like Herbert Marcuse and Erich Fromm, when she offered her 1958 analysis of "world alienation" in *The Human Condition*. In its final chapter we read of capitalist society's obsession with utility and instrumentality, furthered by modern technology, which substitutes a world of machines for the actual world.[13] She points out that in a world driven by instrumentality, whatever we do we are supposed to do in order to make a living and provide for the abundance of goods. The usefulness of things has become their only meaning or value, created "in order to" rather than "for the sake of," in Arendt's words, in an endless chain of means and ends that leads to meaninglessness.[14] We attend university in order to get a job, not for the sake of learning; we work in order to meet our material needs and satisfy our lust for consumption, not for the sake of the work itself. The "worldliness" of human life—constituted by the speech and action essential to public life—is sacrificed on the altar of consumption and wealth accumulation. Perhaps only the artist, because she is compelled by creativity rather than utility and thrives on the means—the "for the sake of"—rather than the end, escapes this endless chain.[15]

We are living in the future Arendt worried about, in a state of technological advancement even she could not have anticipated. Every aspect of our lives undergoes an economic valuation: "time is money"— as is education, creativity, our home, our future, even conversation, friendship, and love. Public activity is reduced to shopping and public space is reduced to the marketplace. In this marketplace, the work that supports and satisfies our seemingly unlimited desire for consumption is valued above the work that builds a non-consumable, durable world— of art, music, ideas, places of beauty. The desire for abundance has defeated the desire for durability, even to the point of sacrificing the earth itself.

We have developed new terms to capture the current, accelerated dynamic between capitalism and technology. Franco Berardi refers to "semiocapitalism" to indicate that capitalist value is no longer simply material but *immaterial*, produced through the tools of mind, language, and creativity.[16] Luis Suarez-Villa calls it "technocapitalism," which he defines as a new version of capitalism founded "on corporate power and its exploitation of technological creativity." If profit depended on the factory production of commodities in the industrial era, it depends now on the commodification of creativity and its inventions. Consider, for example, that creative research is at the center of biotechnology (genomics, biopharmaceuticals), nanotechnology, and molecular computing.[17] Shoshana Zuboff refers to "surveillance capitalism" to name the new logic of accumulation exercised by Google and Facebook, which aim to "predict and modify human behavior" in the name of profit and market control.[18] We also find in use the terms "information capitalism," "digital capitalism," "finance capitalism," and "internet capitalism." All of these terms point to the fact that technology is not neutral or simply functional, as Suarez-Villa points out, but reflects the power, values, and interests of contemporary corporate capitalism.[19]

Once again, we observe, as we did under twentieth-century totalitarianism, the role of isolation and loneliness in a synthesis of forces that can have terrifying effects. It is not unreasonable to claim loneliness is the basic experience of technocapitalism, just as it was of totalitarianism. Our limit case is the lone killer who carries out mass murder, not for a collective political cause a terrorist group would consider just but out of personal rage and resentment. Before we get to that limit, there are less extreme indications of the failure of the social whose outcome is not yet terror but alienation, despair, depression, anxiety, or panic—derivatives, one could argue, of loneliness. We are experiencing the loss of a world in Arendt's sense of a public, political space, but as we undergo dramatic changes to the way we live among others—at home, at work, in love and friendship, in neighborhoods, communities, and cities—we also experience the collapse of the social.

The question is: Are we beginning to feel at home in this desert? To prevent ourselves from adjusting to the worldlessness caused by social failure, we must remember the demand of the lonely: I need to be known, understood, and loved, but I also need to exist for others in the world in order for our life together to be meaningful.

THE TYRANNY OF THE COUPLE

A professor of mine once complained to me of loneliness while living alone in her mid-forties on a street full of families. She described feeling a profound sense of alienation as she watched couples and their children cycle past her house on warm Sunday afternoons and spent long evenings with nothing but television to distract her from too much solitude. At the time, I was a single mother in my early thirties who took for granted that being single was a temporary state and who enjoyed the company of a group of student friends, many of whom were also single. So I understood only vaguely the social critique implied by my professor's reference to "the tyranny of the couple."

Nearly twenty years later I found myself in circumstances similar to hers—in my late forties, single, and a professor, living alone on a street full of families, overcome by feelings of alienation and loneliness. In a few more years I would realize with some surprise that I had spent as many of my adult years single as partnered. This would have been inconceivable to my younger self, not yet aware of normativity and its effects. Marriage and motherhood were a girl's objectives in my community, the prize we did not need to think beyond. My father always said a girl not married by twenty-three is a leftover, but I was confident I had nothing to worry about; at sixteen I had a serious boyfriend, an optimistic collection of dishes and linen, and proficiency in the art of baking pies. Single women in my community were objects of pity and sometimes derision; they were the great unwanted, and neither accomplishment nor personality could release them from their condition. That I would someday join their ranks was as unimaginable as choosing a life of crime.

The "tyranny of the couple" may sound overly dramatic given what we know of political tyrannies, but social norms are also forms of domination. Those who do not fall in line—in this case, single persons—are stigmatized and pathologized. No matter which genders are involved, the intensive idealization of coupledom produces a network of effects that operate invisibly because we don't regard them as absurd or arbitrary. Like members of any majority, couples might be blind to their own status and its associated perks. We do not know if couples actually constitute a majority. Marriage is in decline nearly everywhere across the globe, and the number of single-person households has been on the rise since the 1970s, but this does not necessarily mean there are fewer couples, since couples don't always marry or cohabit.[1] What the decline of marriage does indicate is that our understanding of what it means to live as a couple is changing, and this signals a dramatic shift in values and social habits. It remains to be seen whether intimate love itself will change.

The tyranny of coupledom is caused by its social capital, supported by a lucrative love and sex industry, institutions that sanction marriage and family life, and material benefits. Though both the coupled and the uncoupled experience the effects of this tyranny, the effects are disproportionately felt; some benefit, and some lose, and many benefit in one sense and lose in another.

The couple might experience the terrible disappointment of an unfulfilled promise of happiness or the stress of feigning happiness while they struggle with the reality of domesticity and the effort they are told a relationship demands—or worse, they might experience the domestic violence that privacy permits. To be a couple often means to *perform* coupledom; there is a template to follow, a book of rules. The social, psychological, legal, and economic advantages of sharing life with someone who is loved (at least at the start) are not in every case adequate compensation for the disappointment and the perpetual striving, but the benefits are boosted by the symbolic value of having achieved the status of the normal.

The single person, on the other hand, is assumed to be unhappy and lonely, neither attractive nor loveable enough to be chosen by anyone for an intimate relationship. This assumption is changing but not rapidly enough and not everywhere. Missing from this picture are two obvious perspectives: first, we might prefer to be single; and, second, there is no necessary connection between being single and being lonely. Even if we are single and lonely we should recognize that loneliness is not merely caused by the lack of an amorous relationship; it is *produced* by a complicated network of social practices around coupledom that serve to limit access to care, companionship, and even time and public space for anyone not part of a couple (not to mention access to certain legal and economic benefits). There is no tyranny without support. As Michèle Barrett and Mary McIntosh argue in their critique of the family, if marriage is what everyone wants and needs, we must wonder why it has to be "so massively privileged by social policy, taxation, religious endorsement and the accolade of respectability."[2]

The question, then, is whether single persons would be lonely without a network of social practices to support the centrality of coupledom. This has been a particularly stubborn question for me. I have experienced a complete absence of loneliness when living with an intimate partner to whom I was deeply attached and committed. I have experienced only intermittent loneliness while single but living with my adult son. I have experienced a dull but constant loneliness when living with a partner who was emotionally detached or intellectually incompatible. I have experienced the worst, most intense loneliness when living alone after leaving an intimate partner. But it is important to add that in each case other factors came into play: the presence or absence of close friends who lived nearby, a friendly or alienating workplace, meaningful or unfulfilling work, and even the type of dwelling and city I lived in. Would we be lonely in the absence of an intimate partner if we had networks of care, close friendships, meaningful work, communities and neighborhoods to which we belonged, and homes in which we were not estranged from ourselves?

When we step out of our cultural, normative frameworks, the arbitrariness and absurdity of a society organized around coupledom are exposed. From my own particular vantage point—middle-aged, intellectually inclined, sometimes coupled, now single, a rural to urban transplant living in a cosmopolitan but socially reserved Canadian city— the social habits related to couple normativity that I have come to see as absurd look something like the following.

Couples like to socialize with other couples, and this often means excluding single friends, probably unintentionally more often than not. It could be a gentle tribalism: we wish to spend time with others who have a similar lifestyle as a way to affirm our own choices in life. Perhaps we unconsciously fear that we may all find ourselves alone at some point and want to avoid being reminded of it. Or it could be discomfort with our own pity for the single person at the dinner table who we assume is unhappy and envious.

The single person must accept the couple as a unit. When I invite a friend to dinner who is a member of a couple, I am expected to include the other member of the couple too. But the unit-of-two as standard of measure only applies to couples; no one would feel free to bring a dog, a neighbor, or even a toddler, unless specifically invited to do so.

Couples have a monopoly on time outside of work. A single person might discover that the only friends who will see her on weekends and holidays are single friends. This is because the couple is socially self-sufficient. We are always *at home* with our intimate partners, in the comfort of familiarity, no matter where we are (assuming we are with them because we like them). When we are too exhausted to attend a social event after the workweek, we may still want to go out with a partner because this does not require the same kind of energy. It makes perfect sense that we want to attend events with the person with whom we feel most at home and presumably the person we like the most. But this may leave the single person with limited options if he has no single friends: to attend events alone or not at all.

The time monopoly is particularly obvious on holidays, which can be the bane of any single person's existence. If I complain to my partnered friend about a holiday weekend spent alone, he will tell me in a gesture of solidarity that he and his partner didn't do anything either. He will remind me during the Christmas break that he also hates the holidays, as many people do. But there is a crucial difference between hating the holidays for their commercial noise and false family cheer, and hating them for the isolation and loneliness they impose. I dread major holidays because these are the days during which all the persons I rely on to fill the social needs of my daily life disappear into their own private realms. This includes friends with partners and families, colleagues at work, the owners of my local fruit and vegetable market, the servers and fellow regulars at the cafés I frequent, and even strangers on the street going to work, who form the nameless, yet essential, backdrop to my social world.

When coupled love is valued at the expense of all other forms of love, the latter become stunted through lack of attention and care. This is manifest in a number of ways. One member of a couple might be jealous of her partner's friends. A single woman may not easily develop a close relationship with a coupled man, at least when all involved are heterosexual. When singles become part of a couple, they may abandon their friends. The partner not only becomes the priority but a priority understood as absolute that leaves no room for second or third place. If we are not an absolute priority in another's life—and by this I do not mean we are without friends or love but without a person who puts us first—to find care or help when we need it becomes a challenge. This is especially true as we age.

When we become single after being part of a couple, we can lose the social life we had together. A partner may be lost through divorce or death and with him disappears an entire community of friends, relatives, and acquaintances. In the case of divorce, friends may feel forced to choose sides; in the case of death, the abandonment is more curious. When my mother was widowed in her late seventies, she felt suddenly forgotten by the couples with whom she and my father had socialized for their entire adult lives. It was as though she had died with her husband. The only way I can make sense of this is to consider the absolutely unified nature of the couple, especially in my parents' generation; the couple is a sealed unit in relation to other sealed units. If members of a couple do not cultivate relationships with members of other couples *as separate individuals*, it is reasonable to expect they will not know how to respond to an individual suddenly bereft of her partner. She would remain unknown as an individual; with one half of the unit gone, the other also ceases to exist.

The private realm as we once knew it has all but disappeared in our digital times; we are now involuntary witnesses to the once private life of coupledom on a regular basis. On Facebook, for example, we might be forced to witness the in-house jokes or personal expressions of love and affection between a couple, who inexplicably choose to nurse their love publicly on social media.

We may discover a self-congratulatory dimension to the couple's relation to the single person. Once we have *arrived*—acquired the coveted status of coupledom—even genuine sympathy for the single person's presumed suffering assures the couple that it is best to be coupled; the couple confirms, for their own benefit, that everyone wants what they have. The couple must believe they have made the right choice in life and are deserving of envy; to affirm this envy, they have to assert that single people are lonely.

A similar confirmation occurs when couples who have been together a long time are in the presence of either newly formed couples or divorced persons. The enduring couples are congratulated for achieving, through their own merit, something others either dream of achieving themselves or have failed to achieve. This confirms for the enduring couple that they have done something accolade-worthy, when, in actual fact, the endurance of their relationship might be attributable to any number of mundane factors, with sheer luck thrown into the mix. They might have a high tolerance for boredom, a low tolerance for being alone (which they see as the only alternative to being married), a fierce sense of duty or obligation to a religious or ethnic tradition, or they might not have emotional bonds with other friends, and so on. Possibly, they fear the loneliness of being uncoupled more than others. Marriage is "a refuge from an otherwise unbearable sense of aloneness," Erich Fromm remarks in *The Art of Loving*: "in 'love' . . . one forms an alliance of two against the world, and this egoism *à deux* is mistaken for love and intimacy."[3]

No doubt these absurdities are particular to time and place and may not concur with the experiences of my readers, who will have their own examples. In enumerating these curious social effects of couple normativity, I want to caution the reader that a reflection on coupledom needs to do more than expose a very efficient—if absurd—method of organizing a patriarchal society of workers and consumers that has unfortunate effects on single people. Fromm's "egoism *à deux*" is not always a case of "mistaken" love. Intimate love is not always a myth but one of life's greatest gifts; its real possibilities drive us to search for it. We find evidence of extraordinary amorous attachments throughout history that attest to these possibilities. Anyone who has read the famous twelfth-century love letters between Héloise and Abelard surely finds in them a moving example of the timeless continuity of the emotions involved in intimate, couple-love. There is something unique about this form of love; it has an intensity and attachment that only a rare friendship will match. The difference tends to be a physical one, since we are generally not as physically intimate in friendship as we are in coupled relationships (though the lines between these forms blur). By physical intimacy I do not refer exclusively to sex but include care for a beloved body, which becomes as familiar to us as our own.

Surely we can say that this kind of intimate love is a unique human experience without having to say that those who have not experienced it lead diminished lives? I would argue the love parents might have for their children is also a unique and extraordinary experience but not one that everyone will or ought to have. The love between two very close friends is also exceptional. That such forms of love are inestimable gifts does not negate their vicissitudes. To love and be loved, to be a priority in someone's life, is simply an incomparable experience, and this is true no matter what kind of relationship such love inhabits. The point I am making is that *love* is singular; love itself is the value, regardless of the form in which it appears. From this perspective, the opposite of loneliness is to be without love, not without a partner—a conclusion that liberates us from the fantasy of the couple even as it uncovers new dilemmas.

"Compulsory heterosexuality" and "heteronormativity" were terms coined in the 1980s and 1990s to draw attention to the discriminatory effects of normalizing and universalizing heterosexual relationships and their attendant ways of being. But no one at the time (to my knowledge) thought of investigating the effects of "compulsory coupledom," despite a number of important feminist critiques of marriage and the nuclear family.[4] More recently, however, Elizabeth Brake has coined the somewhat cumbersome term "amatonormativity," from the Latin *amatus* or beloved, to designate "the focus on marital and amorous love relationships as special sites of value."[5] She argues that when we assume it is natural for a human being to enter into an amorous, monogamous, preferential, and permanent relationship with one other person, we carry out "systematic discrimination" against those in non-amorous relationships.

Brake claims that such discrimination is "widely practiced" and accepted without controversy. Those outside of an amorous relationship are subjected to negative stereotyping—judged as immature, irresponsible, undesirable, desperate, or selfish—and to the constant pressure to date and marry. The significant friendships of single people are devalued, even if they provide the material and emotional support that the traditional family is assumed to provide. Amatonormative discrimination operates at the legal and economic levels as well, Brake notes, since singles are ineligible for certain government benefits and reduced insurance rates, have higher living and housing expenses, and face workplace discrimination.[6]

There is a sudden interest in single life in the popular media, particularly among women, and this new public discourse has no doubt buoyed the spirits of those who have felt the stigma of the lonely single person.[7] Bella DePaulo has been for many years a formidable proponent of the choice to remain single. She has made it her life's work to expose discrimination against singles, or "singlism," as she calls it, and more importantly to dissociate the tenacious link between loneliness and solo living by highlighting the quality of life that single persons enjoy. The title of one of her most popular works says it all: *Singled Out: How Singles Are Stereotyped, Stigmatized, and Ignored, and Still Live Happily Ever After*. In this work, DePaulo catalogues examples of singlism from increased sexual harassment, longer hours in the workplace, and invisibility in research studies to frequent accusations of having "no life." She also contests the current media "frenzy over loneliness" and its association with living alone. For every study the new loneliness experts cite that indicates married people are happier and healthier than singles, De Paulo finds one that proves the opposite.[8]

Brake and DePaulo point to a dramatic shift in the normativity of the couple. They contest its monopoly and bring to light alternative approaches to living with or among others, from singles living alone, couples living apart, friends living together to intentional communities.[9] But in DePaulo's pronouncements about the happy single there is a tendency to reverse the initial prejudice. It is empowering to identify with a group that claims victimhood status, but we then risk reinforcing divisions that are merely arbitrary. We should be wary of a minority group that promotes an essentialist identity in order to defend themselves against the essentialist identity of a majority group. Neither couples nor singles constitute a discrete population within themselves; they are not rival sports teams we must cheer on against their opponents.

"Single" is a term only in relation to "couple"; it refers to one aspect of a life, and it has a negative connotation—single is defined by the lack of one particular kind of relationship, an amorous one. If we didn't privilege the couple, we would have no reason to employ these terms. If to be in a couple (as this has been defined for us) or to be single are merely two options among many, and all are valued equally, the only question that matters is whether we are able to give and receive love and care, regardless of what kind of relationships we have. Asking someone why they have never been married would be considered as absurd as asking why they have never been an accountant.[10]

The tyranny of the couple does not operate in a vacuum; it works within a wider social context of work practices, family relations, digital technology, neighborhood and city design, and so on. We must keep this context in mind when we explore the links between coupledom and loneliness. I do not question the centrality and meaningfulness of intimate love in human life; I question the particular institutional form in which love is sometimes housed. We need to ask ourselves whether we are lonely because we are not part of a couple, or because we live in a social environment so impoverished that we must live as couples in order to survive it.

I might add that loneliness is a small price to pay to escape the violence of coupled life. The tyranny of the couple leads to more than social absurdities and economic discrimination; it leads to the most private kind of violence, the victims mostly women. If coupled love protects us from suffering, Lea Melandri points out, it also separates us from others and from the world, enclosing lovers in "an undeniably claustrophobic relation" since they must find one another sufficient just as the mother's body is sufficient for the fetus.[11] The enclosed space of the private might then become a prison for the woman whose all too violable body leaves her vulnerable to the whims or the rage of her lover.

AT HOME

I raised a child by myself. He had a fair-weather father who became an occasional one and finally none at all in any meaningful sense of the term. We moved a lot—too much, as I realized too late. We did not have the village people say we need to raise a child. I left the one that would have rejected me in my new circumstances anyway, and another one did not take its place. I lived in a state of perpetual anxiety about the loneliness that would be my son's if something were to happen to me—an anxiety that has only ebbed in his adulthood.

In his infancy, I was alone with him for the better part of each day. Having just moved to the outskirts of a new city, I had no friends, no occupation other than caregiving, and no regular access to transportation into the city. During the first two years of his life, I had a husband who worked at some distance and at the end of the day lived with us at some distance. The needs of my infant son were both my burden and my salvation. We clung to each other in mutual dependency.

The loneliness of raising a child alone is in a category all by itself. It isn't a matter of too much solitude because I had little time alone. This particular loneliness was born of a devastating isolation in which I was decidedly not alone, in which I bore the psychological weight of being the only person responsible for another life, impressionable and trusting. I was the only one to meet the need that accompanies pure vulnerability—day after day, year after year—in all of its gentle or monstrous incarnations. The loneliness of the single parent is about not sharing an excruciating responsibility.

I longed for relief from this responsibility, giving in to fantasies—of doting fathers, romantic love, and the comforts of family life in the well-lit homes I walked by at dusk, full of books and music and laughter—or so I imagined. I learned for the first time the punishment of ideals.

AT HOME

Emblems of my loneliness: I would go to the mall whenever I had use of a car, just to feel I was still part of the world—a sad statement about the public spaces available to new mothers. I pushed my son in his stroller as though I belonged like the other mothers with strollers and the elderly taking their exercise between Sears and The Bay. I organized a family event for Father's Day with my son's cousins, aunts, uncles, and grandparents. I made a list, itemizing in detail each task required for preparation, drawing out the process so the event appeared more important than it actually was, and would fill more time and space than it actually did. I placed this piece of lined paper in a box of letters and other mementos, thinking that someday I would want a reminder that this is how I once lived, in such a parched social environment that I prolonged the activity of baking and cleaning for two weeks for a family gathering that would be less than enthusiastic and over in three hours.

I discovered this slip of paper one day years later and the loneliness of that time, buried in every mundane item on the list, was released like a stain that reappears after blotting.

I had little idea then of the challenges that awaited me due to the intensity of an emotional bond that isn't shared with another adult and to the fact that I was a mother with a passion for intellectual pursuits. This would demand hours of solitary reading, thinking, writing, and years of sitting in classrooms—all activities incompatible with mothering as it is currently defined. I would echo what Doris Lessing allegedly said to reporters after winning the Nobel Prize for Literature in 2007: "No one can write with a child around. . . . It's no good. You just get cross."[1] A mother's consciousness is divided in two from the moment of giving birth, one part focused on the task at hand, the other preoccupied with another life—where he is at this moment, who is taking care of him, what he is feeling, how to prevent his suffering and precipitate his joy, and how not to ruin his life.

Who will care for the mother alone in her home with a child? Who will replenish her when all is "so lavished and spent" that only a shell of herself remains?[2]

THE ANTISOCIAL FAMILY

I would like to say that my first experience of nuclear family life as an adult crushed any romantic notions I had of it. When my son was born, I experienced the physical and psychological shock of becoming a mother and learning to live with its material consequences—isolation in the privacy of the home and a gendered division of labor that had all kinds of unanticipated ripple effects. This shock is probably still common for new mothers since parenting and homemaking expose unique forms of gender inequality. I had not yet recognized my appetite for intellectual stimulation or acknowledged its incompatibility with mothering; I felt only a vague sense of emptiness and disillusionment. I had imagined slipping easily into the prescribed role of the mother, a role for which I had been primed. Instead, I identified with Edna Pontellier, the protagonist Kate Chopin describes as "not a mother-woman" in her 1899 novel *The Awakening*, for Edna does not idolize her children, worship her husband, or efface her individuality.[1] It had not occurred to me that there was a social context to my isolation and discontent; that there was anything "unnatural" about mothering.

If this first experience of nuclear family life as an adult had in fact crushed my romantic fantasies, would I have tried so hard to create the ideal family a second time? To answer this question, I would have to know what part the fantasy of the ideal family played and what part the reality of social needs played in my desires—the harsh reality of raising a child alone within the particular social context that was mine at the time.

When thinking about loneliness in relation to the family, we need to take this dichotomy between an ideal and the reality of social needs into account. In *How to Live Together*, Roland Barthes points out that if there were not one or two families that "got along well together" we would have no families at all.[2] Like the intimacy of the couple, the family is not *only* a myth; neither is it only a dysfunctional reality. We do find families that thrive, families whose members offer each other emotional and material support, consistent love, care, and companionship. The loneliness experts are no doubt correct in their insistence that family bonds can protect against loneliness and lead to better health. But the family—both as a myth and as a social form—produces loneliness as well, and not only for those without families.

The fantasy of the ideal family appears to be holding its own, despite the potential in families for abuse, neglect, and violence, despite its historical role in reproducing patriarchal norms and class divisions, and despite the fact that nuclear families are now in the minority. Still, we are bombarded with cultural messages that reinforce the centrality of the family to our social existence, to happiness and a meaningful life— from film and television, social media, and religious and government institutions.

This idealism is manifest in a powerful nostalgia. We have lamented family breakdown for decades, memorializing the days when families ate together around the dinner table and siblings stayed in close proximity to one another after they reached adulthood. Many of us still tend to accept that family gatherings should be prioritized over the needs of friends or other commitments and feel a sense of obligation toward family members that we don't to others, especially to provide care (whether or not we fulfill this obligation is another matter). Ethnic groups who maintain strong family ties and traditions may be envied by outsiders who applaud the commitment of these groups to spending time with relatives and caring for aging parents and grandparents, while feeling guilty over their own flagging sense of responsibility for family.

It isn't immediately obvious why we assume the elderly want their children to take care of them or why we might idealize a culture in which families do everything together. Barthes thinks we are fascinated by others who live together harmoniously, a fascination that inspires envy.[3] Perhaps the envy comes first. We want so desperately to believe human beings can live amicably together that we search for it in other people's homes, communities, and cultures. Sometimes we find it but other times what we find is the product of our imagination.

This envy would explain the appeal of, and disillusionment with, Facebook. We regularly complain that Facebook and other social media platforms can generate intense feelings of loneliness. We gaze at profile pictures which often include intimate partners and children. We scroll through innumerable images of smiling couples and families sharing good times—eating together, going to events, travelling, celebrating birthdays, weddings, and anniversaries. Facebook makes voyeurs of us all, and envy is the likely outcome; we witness all that conviviality and want some for ourselves.

Beyond Facebook, we are daily assaulted by stories of life optimization. For example, *The New York Times* features a "Sunday Routine" series that allows the reader a glimpse into the Sunday happiness of "newsworthy" New Yorkers like Neil Patrick Harris and David Burtka. Every detail of their day is documented as an adventure, from getting out of bed together and setting up a pancake bar for their twins, skateboarding in the park, or taking in a Broadway show to spending a cozy evening at home cooking dinner together before putting the twins to bed plugged into their favorite meditation apps.[4] If ours is the age of loneliness, it is also the age of public intimacy. These are perfectly sutured—we peer into the bedrooms and kitchens of others' optimized lives and feel the disappointment of our own.

According to Barthes, the fantasy of living together harmoniously coexists with counter-fantasies of living together badly. He gives two examples: the orphan who discovers he has "a commoner for a father, a rotten family," and the hell envisioned in Sartre's play *No Exit* in which three people are condemned to live in mutual animosity for eternity.[5] But such narratives do not seem to dampen enthusiasm for the belief that the family is the core of our existence and the source of our happiness and fulfillment. Even those who experience the worst families when they are children may fervently believe they will experience their own perfected versions of family life when they are adults.

The potential for disappointment is enormous. Anthony Storr's argument about the overvaluation of interpersonal relationships applies here. We have exaggerated our expectations that intimate relationships should provide happiness, he says; "the burden of value" we have placed on them "is too heavy for those fragile craft to carry."[6] Families themselves suffer from the family ideal, because they expect the family unit to provide all that has been promised to them: happiness, love, safety, and the fulfillment of their social needs. Parents agonize over how to raise their children and feel guilt over their inability to meet the standards set by the industry of best-parenting practices. Those for whom the family fantasy remains out of reach suffer the torment of unsatisfied desires. The profit of fertility clinics is a testament to this torment.

The appeal of the family, however, is not only based on ideals but also on its role in addressing social needs. In the early 1980s, Michèle Barrett and Mary McIntosh summarized the reasons for the family's enduring appeal, a summary still relevant now despite significant social changes in the four decades since. First, they note that the family offers emotional security through a range of experiences that are not available in other social contexts. The fact that we do not choose our families means there is a level of obligation in familial relationships that is not present in others. This sense of obligation means that dependency in the context of the family is acceptable. Young children are dependent on parents, and elderly parents are dependent on adult children. Obligations to siblings or extended family members are not as easy to shirk as obligations to neighbors or strangers. Barrett and McIntosh also point to the familiarity of family relationships; flawed personalities and conflicts notwithstanding, this familiarity provides a certain pleasure—of predictability, of knowing what to expect from one another. Family members love to point out each other's inherited characteristics not only out of interest in genetic inheritance but out of a desire for "tokens of similarity, familiarity and belonging." Family furthermore provides a place for the legitimate expression of emotional need and vulnerability—there is no shame in exposing our weaknesses when we feel at home with people who have taken on some responsibility for us. Included in emotional needs is the need to share "trivial daily anxieties and experiences" with others.[7]

Probably the most important reason for the appeal of the family is its role in raising children. We have for the most part accepted—at least since the 1950s—that the nuclear family is the most effective and efficient social form for raising children. Ideas about what constitutes a nuclear family have changed, but the structure has remained remarkably stable. Two parents are generally assumed to be necessary for a child's well-being (and some would still argue this means a heterosexual couple). This assumption is not without basis, for it is well established that children fare better economically with two parents rather than one. But two seems to be the magic number, a thoroughly normalized family form, despite vast variations historically and culturally, and despite the growing acceptance of the family's mutability. While it might be acceptable now for a same-sex couple to parent a child (at least in Western societies), it would be unusual for a couple to invite an unrelated third person to form a household with them and have an equal say in raising the children.

Given these positive attributes, the family is an effective institution for meeting the social needs of a population. But the family also operates as a powerful ideology, Barrett and McIntosh go on to argue; it perpetuates class hierarchies and a gendered division of labor that is reflected in the world beyond the home—society is "familialized."[8] One of the outcomes of this ideology is that the family has become *antisocial*, a claim that may seem counterintuitive given the family's appeal and its significance for social life. The substance of their argument focuses on the family's monopolization of the comfort, security, and care that human social life necessarily provides for its individuals, and this monopoly means that those who are not members of the best kind of families will most likely find themselves "socially impoverished."[9] Supposedly "a bastion against a bleak society," the family has "made that society bleak"; it is considered "a place of intimacy, but in privileging the intimacy of close kin it has made the outside world cold and friendless." The family is an ideal that "makes everything else seem pale and unsatisfactory."[10]

I imagine this argument will readily appeal to anyone without close family ties or anyone who falls outside the range of the nuclear family ideal and feels excluded from what is considered the norm. On the other hand, I suspect that many who live within a family unit would object to the social privilege Barrett and McIntosh attribute to them, on the basis that there is not enough social or material support for families, especially those with small children. Parents may be emotionally and financially overburdened if they have no extended family or close friends to assist them. The responsibility of parenting, even if it is shared by two people, is strenuous in a social environment in which public discourses on good parenting methods are relentless. A friend recently confessed to me that she feels guilty for not making her toddler laugh enough. I know parents who worry that their two-year-old doesn't say the right number of words yet. The family as a unit can also fall victim to a devastating isolation, even if they have each other.

I am persuaded by the central idea in Barrett's and McIntosh's analysis—that the family is antisocial if we consider its privileged position in a wider social environment—but I disagree with their claim that the family monopoly is the cause and not the effect of an impoverished social environment, for it seems to be both. For those without families or partners, it is no doubt the care and the easy access to companions in a family that provoke envy and intensify the cravings of loneliness. In a family, ideally, there is always company for outings, someone to worry about you, to take you to the hospital if need be, or to cook when you don't feel like it. As forms of sociability and networks of caring relationships dwindle, the family becomes the only available option, and as the family increases in value, other avenues for social fulfillment dwindle further.

I think of the elderly couples I see in hospitals or medical centers. Both members of the couple may be ill and frail, but they must rely on one another, for there is no one else to help them. I think of my mother who cared for my father after a stroke left him prone to violent outbursts for several years. She never told her friends; only her children knew, and we feared for her safety on a daily basis. Care is assumed to come from family—our medical systems depend on it—leaving those without family to care for them much worse off. We might also think about the difficulty we would have in getting involved in children's lives if we were unable or unwilling to have our own, a fact that once again overvalues a specific adult-child relationship and leaves everyone else in a childless world. This raises a host of questions regarding the designs of our homes and communities, and the physical isolation of the nuclear family.

Barrett and McIntosh conclude from their analysis that a social transformation is necessary, one that will spread the benefits normally restricted to families more widely in communities but also create alternatives to marriage and two-parent households, and revitalize public life and the collective organization of care.[11] Missing from their study is a discussion of the more hidden and less measurable elements of the family's appeal, like desire and love, and the choices we make for the sake of these. The family ideal may be a social imperative, but it is not entirely imposed on us; its appeal is not *only* a product of normativity. My response to *The Anti-Social Family* is similar to my response to those who critique compulsory coupledom—these analyses do not always account for love. This is not to say that every family is a loving one; it is to say that we tend to want our living arrangements to center around those we love the most intimately.

Thus, family protects us against loneliness and contributes to the loneliness of others at the same time. The fantasy of the family ideal is as dangerous as the myth of the perfect mother—the source of guilt in those who believe they are failing to live up to its demands and of disappointment in those who realize the falsity of its promise. Socially, the family myth is reproduced through an elaborate apparatus, from government policies and tax laws to social behavioral and moral norms. But beyond the effects of its fantastical elements, actual family life contributes to the loneliness of others in a very concrete sense. This is the fault not necessarily of the family unit itself but of the vast social infrastructure in which it is implicated, organized around work, childcare, education, parenting advice, and housing design.

In reflecting on the appeal of the family—part fantasy, part actuality—I have often wondered how we might live in a social environment not structured around family units. It shouldn't be the case that a person without a family is a person without care. Surely there is another way to live.

AGAINST COMMUNITY

In 2011 eight men from a conservative, reclusive religious community in Bolivia known as the "Manitoba colony" were sent to prison for raping more than a hundred girls and women in their community—no one knows the exact number. The rapes went on for several years, from 2005 to 2009, though this is also in question. The perpetrators allegedly sedated the victims and their families by infusing a drug derived from an anesthetic used on cows through their bedroom windows. The victims woke up in the morning to stained sheets, pelvic pain, and pounding headaches. Some did not remember the assaults; others woke briefly to find a man pinning them down but were unable to move their bodies before they passed out again. They didn't understand what was happening to them—they thought they were dreaming or that the devil was responsible—until one of the rapists was caught entering a bedroom one night in 2009. Only then did the truth emerge.[1]

This is the event that informed Miriam Toews's remarkable novel *Women Talking*, a fictionalized account that focuses on the victimized women meeting in the aftermath of the rapes to decide whether to stay in the community or leave. Ironically, what is most striking in the numerous reports of these crimes is that most of the women apparently did *not* talk. Shame kept them silent; either the young women worried they wouldn't find a husband if they spoke out, or the men with authority in the community persuaded them to stay silent. According to one account, some of the women told their husbands or fathers what had happened to them, and their stories were dismissed as the products of wild female imaginations. But if the reports are accurate, the women did not talk to each other. Even victimized mothers did not tell their victimized daughters what had happened to them.[2] We must ask what prevents the victims of such violation from expressing outrage at the conditions that both led to their victimization and covered it up.

The details of the case are still being contested as I write this. Some argue that the convicted rapists were forced to confess in order to keep secret the widespread incest and rape in the colony. Supporting this theory is the rumor that the rapes continued after the imprisonment of these eight men. The religious leader of the community said that no one understood the crimes. There was nothing "inherent in the colony" that would lead to these rapes, he told a reporter: "There are good people in this world and bad."[3] But his second point does not permit the conclusion that evil actions are always random events. There may be good and bad people in the world, but there are always conditions responsible for nurturing one or the other.

The Manitoba colony in Bolivia is a religious community of Mennonites, an ethnic German Protestant sect originally from Prussia, who settled in Canada (and elsewhere) after fleeing persecution in Russia toward the end of the nineteenth century. They believed in separating themselves from the world, refusing, for the most part, to participate in politics or war. When these immigrants to Canada were required to relax their separate status and send their children to schools where classes were taught in English, the more conservative among them left for Mexico, and then Bolivia and Paraguay—wherever they were permitted to remain reclusive and autonomous. The members of the Manitoba colony keep their distance from the region and its culture: they live hours from the nearest city, Santa Cruz, do not speak Spanish, and their education ends at the age of thirteen for boys and twelve for girls. They do not drive cars, use electricity, enjoy music, sports, or television. Their faith and culture are deeply patriarchal.[4]

Judging from the number of reports on this story, the "ghost rapes of Bolivia," as they are referred to, have incited more than a little fascination, no doubt in part because of the reputation of Mennonites as a quiet, devout, and pacifist people. My own reaction to the story has a different inflection. I do not identify with the Mennonites in Bolivia as "my people," but I share their ethnic and religious heritage, having also descended from the Mennonites who left Russia, though from a group that emigrated more than half a century later. On reading the story, I feel what any outsider might feel reading of such events—sickened by the assaults and the cultivated ignorance and silence that allowed these crimes to continue. But I also feel a kind of rage and revulsion toward the community itself, as one who has experienced living in a similar, if far less orthodox and reclusive, religious community, indoctrinated into the same patriarchal methods of control and the same faith-induced fear of the world. I was protected to some extent from the worst the outside world had to offer—including the possibility of isolation, loneliness, and lack of care—but not protected from the violence within. Trust, faith, innocence, consensus—these provide the very safety that prevents a community's darkest deeds from being exposed.[5]

Community is assumed to be an unqualified good, an ideal social form, universally desired and beneficial to all; it seems as unreasonable to be *against* community as to be against justice or love. The appeal of community seems to derive from the sense of security it ideally engenders through mutual understanding, trust, and care; it mitigates, if not eliminates, loneliness. That we want to belong to a community is therefore easy to understand. Like the family, collective life holds out to us the promise of an enduring, reliable, self-sufficient, and protected social environment, represented for us in television shows, such as *Friends*, *How I Met Your Mother*, *The Big Bang Theory*, or even *Star Trek*, that mimic the family structure or depict its endlessly deferred possibility, though the bond of friendship replaces that of blood. Who wouldn't want this level of trust, support, and especially in the case of *Star Trek*, shared purpose? The community enables us to survive the worst, whether it is heartache from unrequited love or a battle with the Borg.

The community in which I grew up certainly survived the worst. My grandparents' generation—who survived expropriation, imprisonment, torture, rape, and the grief of having to leave behind the dead or imprisoned during the purges of Stalin's terrorizing rule in the 1930s and 1940s—established a community in the new country that promised to keep its members safe from the world. We were protected from worldly temptations (in the 1970s of my youth these boiled down to smoking, drinking, fashion, sex before marriage, and enjoyable sex after marriage). Through a deeply instilled fear of doubting—the work of the devil, we were told—we were also protected from the kind of thinking that resists orthodoxy. It was a foolproof method: seal all avenues of escape by terrifying the children with stories of burning in hell for eternity if they question what is being taught to them.

At twenty, I left this community for the simple reason that its teachings no longer made sense to me and because I longed for the world we so badly misjudged. I would take my chances and risk the potential dangers of the world in order to access its intellectual and cultural treasures; losing the comforts of community seemed a fair price for adventure. It was a spectacular loss—of young friends and adult mentors, the daily fabric of a faith-based life, its song and verse, values, traditions, and shared history—but it was also a spectacular gain.

The loss was perhaps too great to manage at once. I unwittingly sought to fill the gaping hole when I found feminism while a student in the late 1980s. If Ferdinand Tönnies is right in *Community and Society*, the understanding on which a community is founded is one that precedes agreement and disagreement; consensus does not need to be fought for because it is already there, binding community members together.[6] If this understanding does not arise through a deliberative, collective process, it must rest on something else, on a shared identity, on likeness or sameness. It seems the less we belong to a place where we experience solidarity and conviviality with those we happen to live among, the more we turn to identity for a binding agent. I embraced the shared understanding Tönnies speaks of—manifest in the safe space of the building that housed the Women's Studies program at my university. There in the student lounge or kitchen we had animated discussions about whether women should wear makeup or shave their legs and whether men should be allowed into the program. We railed against male philosophers for their indifference or misogyny without bothering to read them and against the professor we deemed not feminist enough (for putting a male author, John Fowles, on the reading list of a course on women and literature). We exulted in being both radical and safe. But it wasn't long before I realized that my new community was as prone to narrow-minded orthodoxy as my religious community. I had exchanged one set of borders, doctrines, and moralisms for another.

We are now hearing a general lament over the dissolution of community in a society turned secular, transient, urban, competitive, financialized, and alienated from family. At the same time, the word "community" has become ubiquitous, applied indiscriminately to any identity group to which we feel we belong, whether springing from religion, ethnicity, ideology, activism, or online activity. Chance communities—those that are formed simply because of proximity, like a neighborhood, or out of shared interests and activities—are being replaced by communities founded on a shared identity. But the identity we discover in our pursuit of the ideal community "never really existed in the first place," says Franco Berardi.[7] The issue is not that we don't have an identity—we have many—but that we don't have the pure identity that our desire often invents for us and that binds us to others whom we want to believe share in this pure identity.

In other words, what binds us to an identity is a lie. This is Kwame Anthony Appiah's point in *The Lies That Bind: Rethinking Identity*, which opens with the observation that, historically, identity was not the social catch-all it is today; no one until the middle of the twentieth century would have declared their race, sex, or class as an identity—rather, identity was "utterly particular and personal." He gives the example of George Eliot's *Middlemarch* protagonist Rosamond, who feels she is losing her identity because she discovers the man she loves is in love with someone else.[8] I do not suggest we never need to identify with this or that social classification (women would never have won the right to vote if this were the case) but to recognize that we are not determined by these classifications.

When a community is based on a social classification that determines who we are, it must define itself in distinction from others, which necessarily implies isolating itself from outsiders. This is when the community becomes antisocial. When we refer to *the* Muslim community (or Jewish, Christian, etc.) or *the* LGBTQ community (or Black, feminist, Indigenous, etc.), we imagine each of these groups as homogenous, as inclusive only insofar as they are exclusive—betrayed by the telltale definite article. The irony we tend to ignore is that inclusivity requires the very exclusivity it purports to fight. For example, the more letters we add to the original acronym LGB (extended now to LGBTQIA, LGBTQ2S, or LGBTTQQIAAP), the more sense it makes to simply refer to what the designation excludes: All But Straight, or perhaps more precisely, All But Cis and Straight, with a pithy acronym of ABCS. But this would mean stressing the exclusionary function of inclusiveness, which we would all like to deny.

If we have lost a place to which we belong, our longing for community may grow more nostalgic; our desire turns it into a paradise lost, as Zygmunt Bauman suggests, not a paradise we know from experience but one we assume has occurred in the past.[9] Like the ideal family, the community we long for is imagined and very little like the actual lived experience of community; our feeling of lack inflates its mythic proportions and intensifies our desire for it.

The lesson of the Manitoba colony is clear: the paradise we long for can become a prison. When we insulate ourselves from the world, we insulate ourselves from the inspiration and disagreement necessary for pluralism, from the crucial checks and balances on authority, from the thinking that continually undoes the thinking of the day before,[10] and from freedom itself. Incest, figuratively speaking (but also literally), is given free reign.

When I hear a demand for safe space—common now among various social justice groups—I feel the claustrophobia I felt in my youth. There is no such thing as an absolute, safe space—human beings are always both vulnerable to the cruelty of others and capable of being cruel—but neither is an ideal safe space an absolute good. We take precautions, of course; we want to protect ourselves and others from violence and cruelty, but we must also protect ourselves from too much protection. This is the principle of immunity, as Roberto Esposito explains in his provocative analysis of a global politics obsessed with security. We know how necessary the body's immune system is to ward off disease, but we also know that if carried beyond a certain threshold, immunity can become autoimmunity and attack the very body it is supposed to protect.[11] We must immunize ourselves against too much immunity.

Too much immunity leads to an obsession with threat, as we know during these days of border walls and detention centers. To protect the community from the threat that lies outside its borders is exhausting work and the more effort put into this protection, the greater the threat appears. This is Bauman's insight. The community, he argues, will ultimately heighten rather than mitigate its members' *insecurity* since it calls for the daily vigilance and struggle demanded "to keep the aliens off the gates and to spy out and hunt down the turncoats in [its] own midst." Ironically, he adds, it is only through this "sword-brandishing" that the feeling of being part of a community can be kept alive.[12] The community founded on a preestablished understanding only feels its privileged warmth and belonging because of this vigilance against the outside. This is why the assimilation of feminist work into mainstream academic disciplines has threatened the existence of Women's Studies programs that were so crucial in their early days and why the assimilation of my religious sect into the world it once carefully held at bay has, over the years, eroded the deep bonds of the community. It is the very safety of the community that fosters the fear of the outside and becomes unintentionally suffocating, operating as a "voluntary ghetto," Bauman says. The safer the insiders feel, "the less familiar and more threatening appears the wilderness outside, and more and more courage is needed to venture past the armed guards."[13]

We are caught in the dilemma of longing for a community that once acquired in the absolute form we desire would demand too much from us. Bauman explains the dilemma: human beings crave both freedom and security. The price we pay for the privilege of being in a community is individual freedom—to think, act, and behave as we choose regardless of others' thoughts, actions, and behavior— to be authors of our own lives. The price we pay for being without a community is the security of living among a trusted group of people who will care for us and with whom we share an understanding despite occasional conflict. Though we may never be able to resolve this dilemma, Bauman says, we will continue to try: "Being human, we can neither fulfil the hope nor cease hoping."[14] At the heart of this trade-off is loneliness, always quick to accompany freedom. The one who leaves the community for the sake of freedom is bound to face loneliness. We have to wonder whether fear of the world and hostility toward it are worse.

Despite brilliant critiques by such thinkers as Kwame Anthony Appiah, Amin Maalouf, Amartya Sen, Gayatri Spivak, and an entire contingent of post–Second World War European philosophers who knew well the dangers of collectives based on an identity considered pure, the demand of community for a foundational identity has only intensified, bringing with it violent excesses. The fundamental problem these critiques expose, as Amartya Sen puts it, is "the implicit belief in the overarching power of a singular classification." It is a belief, he adds, that "can make the world thoroughly inflammable."[15] The very same community members who are good to one another can become the community members who throw bricks into the windows of immigrants coming from elsewhere.[16]

In another version, as the Manitoba colony reveals, the bricks are thrown inside the house. My grandmother knew who in our Mennonite community had once turned their neighbors in to the authorities in the old country, who had assisted the Nazis or the roving communist bandits, and who had turned their backs on the starving children begging at their doors. There was anti-Semitism, racism, and class arrogance alongside compassion and generosity even in the good times; in the bad times, kindness was thin, overshadowed by a very legitimate fear—evidence of the marriage of terror and isolation that Arendt found so compelling.

This is the terror of collective life. As soon as we create community, it becomes a territory in need of defending. There has to be a way to defer the closure, to construct permeable borders that prevent imprisonment and the violence engendered by too much protection. There may be no way to resolve the dilemma Baumann explicates between the longing for freedom and the longing for security, in which case we must find a way to live that fully satisfies neither.

NOSTALGIA

I read my father's life story at his funeral service, standing at the pulpit of a church packed with people, most of them from the religious community I left over thirty years before. I am used to standing at the front of lecture halls with a hundred or more students, but it was a unique experience speaking about my father to people who knew him and who knew me as a child. There was my Sunday school teacher, the boy I had a crush on when I was ten, and the people who owned neighboring farms. There were my father's friends of some seventy years or more, who witnessed every milestone in his life—his wedding, the death of his parents, the birth of four children, anniversary celebrations, a forced retirement due to a stroke, and finally, the end of all milestones. Their faces were full of kindness and sympathy; they flooded the church and my parents' home with flowers and cards, a testament to their respect and affection for this man who was my father.

The loneliness I had felt in the two months before his death, as I helplessly watched him withdraw from life and faced the world's seeming indifference, was compounded by this powerful display of community feeling and support. I was overcome by an intense wave of nostalgia and lamented the loss of the community I left. With sudden clarity, I understood the price I had paid for my restless movement from one city to another, feeling as though I had insufficiently valued the benefits of longevity in love and friendship. My parents were married nearly fifty-eight years and suddenly this felt like the most important achievement in life. I wanted to crawl back into my childhood and do everything differently.

Nostalgia is peculiar; it is not only a longing for what we had in the past—childhood security, a close community, passionate love—but a longing for a glossier version of that past. When we lose someone or something, nostalgia creeps in and may grow stronger over the years. The lost object is polished over time until it glows and bears little relation to what it once was. We forget there are very few fine things in life that are not tinged with something less fine; there are always trade-offs to be made.

The nostalgia sparked by my father's funeral dissipated over the next few weeks as I remembered my experience of the stifling nature of this same community, its demand for conformity and moratorium on thinking, its tendency to moral hypocrisy and judgment, and its patriarchal methods of control. I remembered I had left because the sacrifice demanded in return for the security of the community was thinking and acting as an individual. This does not negate the value of its support or deny the genuine kindness of many good people within it but recognizes that for some of us the sacrifice is too great.

The Farewell is a 2019 film that tells the story of Billi, a young Chinese American woman, grappling with the news of her grandmother's diagnosis of terminal illness and with the family's decision—faithful to Chinese custom—to keep this a secret from the dying woman. Billi and her parents travel to China to visit *Nai Nai* for a family wedding, though this is a ruse to get the extended family together one last time.

Throughout the film, we experience with Billi, and to some extent with her father, who is also ambivalent on the question of informing Nai Nai of her cancer, the emotional turmoil caused by the family's reasons for keeping Nai Nai's diagnosis a secret from her. The rationale is explained by Billi's uncle: if they keep silent, the family will experience all of the relevant emotions for Nai Nai and leave her free to enjoy her remaining days. During a tense exchange over a family dinner we are privy to the clash of cultures as Billi's parents defend their choice to leave China after being told they should have stayed with Nai Nai—the clash of collectivism versus individualism that typically symbolizes the difference between East and West.

At one point during this dinner, Billi erupts in anguished resentment toward her parents for taking her away from the extended family and all that she knew—Nai Nai's house where she spent happy summers—to be a lonely family of three in America. This scene and the fact that despite the torment it causes her, Billi does not tell her grandmother of her diagnosis, seem to convey the message that Billi's parents did indeed sacrifice too much. The story draws us into the family's experience, and we feel with Billi the loss of close family ties. It is tempting to side with the extended family's position—the individual must sacrifice her wishes for the sake of the collective in order to benefit from the life of the common.[1]

I have so often had the opposite wish, that my parents had taken us from all we knew, for the sake of the freedom to make judgments as thoughtful individuals rather than relinquish autonomy and responsibility to a higher authority.

"THE SOUL AT WORK"

In the news on September 17, 2018: Amazon is among the biggest employers of workers who receive food stamps in the United States—nearly one in three workers in the state of Arizona, for example.[1] According to the Trades Union Congress of the UK, CEO Jeff Bezos earns in one second what a warehouse employee makes in five weeks.[2] Low pay is only the tip of the iceberg: in Amazon's cavernous warehouses workers are subjected to stringent surveillance measures, working under a point system that penalizes them for any "idle time," missed "productivity targets," and even illness. To ensure an efficient work environment, employees are prohibited from talking to coworkers and encouraged to participate in the surveillance through an anonymous assessment system; these assessments are taken into account in management decisions about who gets to stay and who must leave.[3] Although effective for worker control, surveillance failed to save 48-year-old Billy Foister from dying of a heart attack, unnoticed where he lay on a warehouse floor for twenty minutes.[4] Here is organized loneliness in full swing.

I borrow the title of this piece from Franco Berardi, who elaborates a new form of alienation in the digital age that departs from the alienation Marx analyzed in *The Economic and Philosophic Manuscripts of 1844*, his early essays on labor, profit, and the power of money under the capitalist system. "Alienation" (*Entfremdung*) is the term Marx uses to describe the detachment and lack of autonomy that define the relationships of the industrial worker to the products she makes, to the labor she carries out to make them, to her coworkers, and even to her own humanity. She is detached from her labor because it is surrendered to the factory owner, and from herself since her labor has nothing to do with her personal interests or talents. In fact, the moment she has no compelling reason to carry it out she shuns work "like the plague." Since she has only her own labor to give, she is reduced to a commodity; the more productive she is, the more she increases the profit and power of the capitalist and the more alienated she becomes, for she is never a subject or person in this process—she is denied both dignity and autonomy. If there is an oversupply of labor, Marx warns, she may succumb to worse: "beggary or starvation."[5]

The industrial worker is alienated from the objects he manufactures—for he could never own them himself—at the same time that he is enslaved by them, for he depends on his wages to meet his basic needs. The object takes on a value that the worker does not have. The diamond miner, for example, can never afford the precious stones he extracts. Marx captures the irony: "labor produces for the rich wonderful things—but for the worker it produces privation. It produces palaces—but for the worker, hovels. It produces beauty—but for the worker, deformity."[6]

Given these conditions we might be surprised by Berardi's provocative reference to the relative freedom of the soul in the industrial era. He claims that in the history of capitalism the body of the worker was disciplined but the soul was left alone; the industrial worker was still free to do what he wished with his intellectual and emotional life, for this life was not of interest to the industrial capitalist.[7] In fact, the workers' common experience of alienation fostered solidarity and the possibility of rebellion; they were capable of building a community on the basis of their very alienation from capitalist interests.[8]

For Amazon warehouse workers, and for millions of workers who today carry out demeaning industrial labor in the poorest parts of the world, Marx's analysis has lost none of its incisiveness; the warehouse, like the sweatshop, reduces workers to commodities, enslaved by their need for wages and consumer demand for cheap products, convenience, and speed. But digital technology has changed the nature of work for many of us in the richest parts of the world. The "cognitariat"—Berardi's adaptation of Marx's "proletariat"—are the workers who spend their days engaged in various forms of mental labor while performing identical physical activity—sitting before screens and moving fingers across a keyboard.[9] Typing is the physical definition of work today for everyone from the architect and travel agent, software developer and lawyer, to the professor and student. But what cognitive work demands of us is creativity; rather than material objects, work now produces projects, styles, and ideas. This is a unique feature of a hyper-technologized capitalism—the "colonization" of a dimension of life and work neglected by previous versions of capitalism. As Luis Suarez-Villa points out, creative research in such fields as biotechnology, nanotechnology, and molecular computing is now at the center of the commodification process. Transformed by commercialization, creativity is being subsumed into the workday. But these are at cross-purposes, as any artist who has had to please a state or public would know, for "the commodification of creativity often carries the seeds of its destruction."[10]

The demand of cognitive labor for these creative, innovative, and communicative energies changes our relation to the workday. The work of the cognitariat is not the labor left joyously behind at the end of an industrial workday, since the cognitive worker does not necessarily leave her work at the end of the day. She is prevented from maintaining a private life not only by electronic devices but also by the nature of cognitive work that demands what Berardi believes are "the best part of [her] intellectual capacities."[11] She begins to value work as the most interesting aspect of her life and no longer opposes the extension of her workday—in fact, she may choose it.[12] How do we explain this shift from the industrial worker's discontent with his exploitation to the cognitarian's acceptance of the exploitation of her time and creativity? Berardi thinks economic need is an insufficient explanation; we must also take into account the loneliness and monotony of contemporary metropolitan life.[13] As wealth comes to mean accumulation and consumption rather than "the simple capacity to enjoy the world available in terms of time, concentration and freedom," and competition makes enemies of us all, we lose what he calls "the eros in everyday life"—eros interpreted broadly here to mean pleasure in the affectivity and communication of human relations.[14] We invest desire in our work because there is nowhere else for it to go. We define ourselves on the basis of work achievements and the worth of a life on the basis of productivity because we have nothing else. The outcome is an antisocial existence: the more we work, the less time we have to be together with others; and the less we are together with others, the more we fall back on work to fill our time. Work becomes what we do because there is no one with whom we can do something other than work. As work subsumes life, life outside work dries up; the social landscape turns into desert.[15]

In Berardi's view, the new alienation in the digital age is caused by the exploitation of our souls. What he means by "soul" might strike a reader as ambiguous; it is not the seat of intellectual life but something both material and metaphorical.[16] He describes the soul variously as "a vital breath" or energy that transforms biological matter into an animated body, as a "sensibility" that opens the body "sympathetically towards the other," and as language and relation itself.[17] This "vital breath" is evidently not the exclusive property of one body, therefore not the source of mind or personhood; the vital breath is always-already relational.[18] The soul thus symbolizes a dimension of life composed of the affective, mental, and sensuous forces that orient us toward others. We are not mere bodies that act together mechanically or mere minds that think in total isolation; we are souls—sensible to one another, responsive, communicative, and empathic. This sensible and sensitive dimension of life is now being put to work, harnessed to market forces via the tools of technology.

The new cognitariat is unable to wrest the soul free from enslavement; gone is the freedom once enjoyed by the industrial workers to discuss autonomy and revolt when not at work. This is ironic: the cognitive work we thought freed us from the monotony of manual labor now subjects us to a mental captivity even the industrial worker was able to escape at the end of the day—and we comply, taking work with us wherever we go with our digital devices in hand, though we complain incessantly about never being able to leave work behind. Tethered to our smartphones, our cognitive labor becomes detached from a social world of bodies we no longer meet.[19]

No wonder workplace loneliness has become a popular topic of public discussion. Our devotion to the flexibility and convenience technology offers to us (or to our employers) produces isolation—by design. Consider the latest trend of "hot desking"—when office workers no longer have their own desks to work at but rotate among a number of desks and spaces on a first-come, first-served basis. From the employer's perspective hot desking saves costs; since not everyone is in the office at the same time, no space is left unused. Businesses also allege the practice improves interaction among a greater number of coworkers, which increases productivity, creativity, and efficiency. But apparently many are unhappy with hot desking, preferring a work space that can be personalized with plants or photographs on a desk, and snacks in a drawer, as well as a more regular rapport with those at neighboring desks—as though we create a home or a very small neighborhood at work, a familiar, predictable space to call our own. We could consider other workplace changes: communication occurs through texting and email rather than face-to-face; the use of headphones imposes a kind of solitary confinement—we are alone with our screens; longer hours or part-time hours eliminate any after work social hours; or the flexibility of work may mean there is no office to go to at all.

When we do not congregate often or easily at work, we lose a specific social form of interaction that we may not realize we need until we are without it. A real estate agent, for example, whose paperwork is now exclusively digital, may lament having no office to go to; he misses having to leave home for another place where he can chat with fellow agents over a morning coffee after hanging up his coat and checking his mailbox. A young NGO member who only meets her busy coworkers once a week for two hours spends the remainder of the week in complete isolation, perhaps mystified by the source of her feelings of emptiness, because this is all that she knows. Cafés are crammed with office-deprived start-ups avoiding the isolation of working at home. Their baristas are lonely and bored, working in the library-silence of these once lively public spaces. The new gig economy epitomizes this work homelessness—the Uber driver and the DoorDash dasher are not even classified as employees and have no workplace or workmates. They are promised the freedom of work conditions that mimic self-employment—independence and the choice of hours—according to DoorDash, "the freedom to dash anywhere."[20]

Without a common space to inhabit that facilitates the interactions of bodies, we no longer experience the unique social exchange of the workplace, however fraught with personality clashes, office politics, or banal chitchat. Imperfect and idiosyncratic, the workplace demands our bodily presence and our civility, and provides a place to which we belong. Our work colleagues are not necessarily our best friends, but they familiarize a space we daily inhabit; they become persons for whom we extend a certain amount of care and interest, even if they are limited to a specific social context. That these relationships may end after changing jobs or retiring, eliminating the context that held them together, does not lessen their meaningfulness during the time that a workplace is shared.

"THE SOUL AT WORK"

The history of the concept of alienation may be full of ambiguity—Arendt, Hegel, Kafka, Fromm, all mean different things by it, and even Marx defines it in a number of conflicting ways,[21] yet whenever I teach Marx's essay on alienated or estranged labor, I find among the students an intuitive understanding of alienation as a sense of futility when working at a meaningless job, accompanied by the need to cut off some vital dimension of themselves in order to carry on. They have their own examples of alienating summer jobs and I give them mine: working on a fruit farm after mechanization. Farmwork has always consisted of hard physical labor, but before mechanization, it was also social. In the cherry orchard my sister and I worked as a team picking fruit from the same tree, we could talk and laugh, and flirt with the boys from the city assigned to the next tree. In the peach-packing shed, before loud machinery cut us off from one another, the women and girls who worked together for the six-week harvest stood side by side and exchanged news and gossip. But the new mechanized packing table required us to stand facing the back of the next peach-packer; the machinery prohibited movement and conversation, which greatly pleased my father whose objective was to increase productivity, not conviviality. Work became monotonous and antisocial; we lived for our weekends.

The meaninglessness of work arises from this antisocial character, as well as a lack of autonomy; when work does not require our creative initiative, personal interest, agency, or self-expression, it does not engage us. The workplace then becomes a place in which one has to perform a role. In a 2009 study of a global management consulting firm in London, one manager likens her workplace to a masquerade party. She dons a mask on entering and removes it at the end of the day. A young consultant at the same firm—bookish and creative—calls his work "asphyxiating" and "brain-rott[ing]" because it demands time but little intellectual effort. He and his coworkers complain of parched social lives, their corporate personas displacing the person they were free to be outside of work. As one employee complains, if life consists only of dull work and sleep, there is nothing interesting to talk about with others.[22]

The heart of the problem is the *almost* inescapable entanglement of work in capital. The meaning of work is reduced to an activity performed in order to collect wages necessary for survival, when it could mean an activity of sustained effort or exertion related to what we can offer the world through our talents and interests. Arendt warns of the transition to a "society of jobholders"—simultaneously a society of consumers—in which all human activities are reduced to "securing the necessities of life and providing for their abundance."[23] In a prescient passage, she urges us to consider that the society of jobholders demands we abandon our individuality—"the still individually sensed pain and trouble of living"— and accept the automatic, "tranquilized" behavior expected of us. With this pronouncement she speculates that the modern age, though it began with such promise and activity, "may end in the deadliest, most sterile passivity history has ever known."[24]

In classrooms I used to give my academic work as an example of activity kept free from the market, neither alienated nor instrumental and certainly not tranquilized or passive. My meaningful attachment to the means and ends of my work would be impossible for the industrial worker or the corporate employees quoted earlier. I would comment on the relatively benign, if irritating, institutional aspects of academic life that less than two decades ago prevented the more meaningful work of thinking, writing, and mentoring. For the most part, I did not feel that my working life was detached from life itself, nor did I have to surrender my autonomy or talents to an authority that required me to be someone other than who I was. My research and teaching projects were motivated exclusively by interest—I was as far from market concerns as anyone could be.

This example—or any equivalent example of work that manages to escape instrumentalization and financialization—leads to an interpretation of "the soul at work" that deflects Berardi's critique by noting the ambiguous distinction between life and work. We typically do pit work against life when work is considered a mere means to the end of more meaningful activities like social interaction, the pursuit of a passion, or leisure activities. When work is central to what we find most valuable in life, however, we are not so quick to make this distinction. In this sense, putting the soul to work is the very enactment of freedom rather than enslavement. Work that demands the engagement of our souls—our emotions, sensitivities, and creative sensibilities—does not have to mean the soul is exploited. Recall Anthony Storr's insistence that our projects matter, not only our intimate relationships. We are social creatures, but we also have an extraordinary capacity for throwing ourselves into an endeavor that takes us beyond ourselves. Becoming wholly absorbed by a project—writing a book, designing a building, founding an organization, starting a band—may be among the most exhilarating (if torturous) experiences in life. The singular focus one needs to carry out such projects demands that distractions be eliminated. We may choose our work over a social event; we may choose solitude, and indeed, loneliness, over company in order to work.

But the difference between creative work that engages one's passions and talents and consequently escapes the constraints of market capitalism, and the work carried out in Amazon's warehouses or on the streets by dashers is so vast that we have to question the meaning of the term "work." There are conditions for the work I love that render it antithetical to the work carried out by the vast majority of people in the world, conditions that are now under threat: autonomy, creativity, and the authority to make independent judgments and craft new ideas, as well as unrestrained time—not having to work under overwhelming pressure (the rarest of these conditions). Creative work like writing and carrying out research are the greatest pleasures, if also the most mentally taxing, but there are a host of other activities I call work that are also meaningful when they are tasks that contribute to the promotion of learning. At work, I am a part of something I believe in. It is no coincidence that the further my work is from market considerations, the more interesting and satisfying it is.

This love of work only confirms Berardi's argument. When work is not carried out to serve the needs of capital, it is an affirmation of life. When work has a value beyond an economic one, a prolonged workday does not mean we are complicit with the forces that demand ever more from us. We may love our work because we can devote ourselves more fully to it in ways we could not historically—I'm thinking in particular of women here—given we spend less time on taking care of basic necessities. This is what freedom from household labor, including full-time childcare and eldercare, and other time-consuming tasks, has allowed us; we can immerse ourselves more fully into the work we love. In this case, work does not negate but intensifies "the eros in everyday life."

The conditions of my work are changing, however, as corporate interests and technology transform higher education. Academics are not the factory workers whose bodies merge with a machine for eight monotonous hours a day for the profit of the capitalist, but we are becoming one with a corporate machinery that forces our mental activity to bend to its purpose: ideas must have a monetary value, teaching practices must be streamlined, lecture content made palatable, learning outcomes guaranteed, and grades negotiated like sales items. The authorities to whom we surrender our talents and creative energies are administrators (increasingly, business experts rather than scholars) and a student body pressured by fear and competition into trading an education for job training—for which they can hardly be blamed. It is a dark time for literature and languages, art, music, and theatre, history and philosophy—suddenly considered superfluous in a financialized world where all value must be quantifiable.

The shutting down of departments in the arts and humanities testifies to the fact the university has become a unique kind of battleground in the conflict between corporatism and creativity, since it represents the best of creativity and independence of thought, neither of which can survive commodification. Thought is inherently creative; it demands a social context in which new ideas, however contentious, are encouraged.[25] The university is supposed to provide such a context. If we do not win this battle, then who will? But we are not winning. The demand for efficiency and productivity is increasing, bringing with it more administrative work, less face-to-face contact and conviviality, and fewer opportunities for the exchange of ideas.

The most obvious sign of the battle we are losing is the rapid increase in contract instructors who cost far less and teach far more than permanent faculty, who have little time for research, and who are not permitted to contribute to an enduring institutional culture due to short-term contracts. They underpin the entire system, moving almost namelessly from institution to institution, contract to contract, often unable to establish roots, family lives, or scholarly reputations. They are peripheral to the departments in which they work since their voices do not count in decision-making and the future culture of their temporary stations. The distinction between permanent faculty and contract instructors is absolutely clear, the new upstairs–downstairs situation that both unions and administrations block anyone from changing. The social implications are devastating: without roots, permanence, or time, friendships cannot be made, which renders solidarity impossible, and without solidarity, the conditions of working life cannot be contested. Competition is the new fearmonger of the twenty-first century; it keeps everyone isolated and working so hard that there is no time to act together. Even if there were time, the system we struggle against is so pervasive it requires a unity of masses across all institutions, and we no longer know how to inspire such unity.

To fight the destruction of intellectual life at our universities, we would have to talk to one another and embark on a course of action together. But like other workplaces, the academic institution produces isolation rather than solidarity. Disciplines and departments are often described as silos because they must compete against one another for funds and recognition. As the number of enrolments and administrative positions rise, space becomes a premium and common rooms for human interaction a low priority. Even if we had such rooms, we would need the time and inclination to use them. Lunch is no longer a break from work but an accompaniment to email time, "eating al desko" according to a recent *Guardian* article.[26] Increased course management tasks and the flexibility to carry them out anywhere with internet access mean that we work in our offices less and less. On the surface, the effect on students seems negligible, as face-to-face meetings are considered more of an inconvenience than an opportunity.

This is because they *are* an inconvenience at a time when students are perpetually overwhelmed and not only by their studies and having to work to pay for them; they are assaulted by the relentless demands of social media and the distractions of the digital sphere, which seem impossible to avoid. Course assignments plunge many of them into a paralyzing anxiety or panic. As a result, the majority become resistant to reading anything longer or more complex than a Wikipedia entry. The inevitable outcome of this predicament is a prohibition on thinking as provocation rather than as cognitive exercise, and without provocation, learning cannot occur. Instead of acting as gadflies—the name Plato gave to Socrates because of the stinging effect of his challenges to prevailing opinions—we who teach these youth act as facilitators or service providers. We do not seek to understand the root cause of their paralysis—indeed, if we do, we feel as overwhelmed by it as they do—but try to make everything easier for them in an atmosphere in which to challenge means to offend.

There is no division between their studying and their working lives; both are carried out as instrumental activities related to an income now or in the future. I have heard conscientious students confess to guilty feelings when they spend time with their friends rather than studying on a day when they are not at their paid jobs. They are as driven by, and as proud of, their productivity as faculty. Who can blame them, for they are promised a bright future at the same time that they are inundated with news of crisis and disaster. The belief in their own singular gifts falters in the face of the unforgiving, competitive environment that society has cultivated throughout their childhoods. The relentless pressure to achieve when only a few will be rewarded is surely the source of rising rates of anxiety and psychological breakdown in our student populations. It would be difficult to separate loneliness from anxiety and depression, for they go hand in hand. Who can find friends among competitors? Who has time for friends when daily life is crowded with work, study, and the maintenance of a virtual persona?

We who cling to the lifeboats our meaningful work offers us are the lucky ones. For the rest, there is the slow adaptation for which human beings are famous. Necessity is given a positive spin for the sake of surviving an otherwise intolerable situation. In an airport once, I watched a woman given the unenviable task of directing impatient, bored people through security transform an otherwise tedious process with her sense of humor and lively exchanges with those passing through. In a local grocery store, I witness a cashier caring for her regulars, including a mentally ill woman who frequents the store. A barista in a busy café, once given some responsibilities, comes to care about his workplace as though he owns it; he has a sense of pride in the place. What seems clear to me is that those who find meaning at work find it through their relationships with those they serve and feel a sense of their own contribution to a public world. They take pride in this contribution. We are greedy for dignity, grasping at the smallest opportunities to procure it. But as long as our work activities are tied to necessity, squeezing out its antithesis—life itself—these small moments of enjoyment are nothing more than an adjustment to meaningless work no one should have to make.

For the lucky ones, too, however, there is adjustment to the relentless demands of accelerated time in the name of productivity and achievement—time no longer easily pried free from the market. As Berardi warns us, intellectual work is increasingly absorbed into the domain of economic production; we are required to transform "every fragment of mental activity" into capital and with ever greater speed.[27] Productivity becomes the value—above the ethical and political matters that once preoccupied intellectuals—above the life of the mind, which tends to develop slowly, and only in the absence of pressure or promise of reward. The needs of the market overwhelm the needs of intellectual life: solitude, time for thinking and creating, and a public space for the discussion of ideas. Alienation sets in; our souls are being put to work, which means thought and feeling, relation and language, creativity and imagination are no longer free. We join the ranks of the great overwhelmed as our student numbers swell, as the pressure to win grants robs us of the time to think, and as we too become isolated and lonely. Under these conditions, we may despair over an institution that cares less and less about the critical interrogation of our times and a philosophical establishment that falls silently in step. Those of us who have made the university our work-homes solely on the basis of our appetite for learning may begin to feel we are strangers on its doorstep.

Work speaks to the public and private conditions of loneliness that I have been moving between. Most of us participate in a common world through our jobs, and ideally, through the exercise of our talents and engagement of our interests. If work does not provide us with a social environment, if it leaves us isolated at our jobs, we will spend a good portion of our days lonely. If work does not provide us with the opportunity to contribute meaningfully to a common world, we will experience the alienation that shadows loneliness.

It is safe to conclude from the current conditions of working life— insecurity, isolation, precarity, competition, and the exploitation of time and creativity—that we are witnessing the ravaging of the world that Arendt predicted would be the outcome of isolation. It is a social catastrophe and even if we are lucky enough to escape its most brutal effects, we are all affected indirectly.

IN THE DESERT

How will we know we are in a desert if the desert is all that we know?

In *The Myth of Sisyphus*, written in 1940 "amid the French and European disaster,"[1] Albert Camus describes a lucid encounter with the absurdity of our habitual lives:

> It happens that the stage-sets collapse. Rising, tram, four hours in the office or factory, meal, tram, four hours of work, meal, sleep and Monday, Tuesday, Wednesday, Thursday, Friday and Saturday, according to the same rhythm—this path is easily followed most of the time. But one day the "why" arises and everything begins in that weariness tinged with amazement.[2]

For Camus, it is only when we face the absurdity of existence—the fact that there is no absolute meaning or purpose provided for every individual life and there is nothing to console us for this lack—that we can live freely. This is why "amazement" tinges our weariness over habitual life. It signals the beginning of living a life fully in the present and abundant in experiences—at once rebellious, passionate, and free. Only when we encounter and embrace freedom in the face of absurdity do the props that support the theatre of our habits and norms—the "stage-sets"—collapse.

I thought of this passage often during a time of unbearable alienation teaching in a department in which, for one reason or another, I never felt at home. Using Camus's formula I constructed my own catalogue of weariness, structured around administrative work, lecture preparation, student consultation, teaching, email, research, and sleep, all "according to the same rhythm." But I had the faculty position coveted by every PhD graduate, the job security that almost no one has anymore, and a salary that put me in the company of the economically privileged—I felt I had no right to the despair that overwhelmed me.

I only realized later, once I took up a position at another university, that the changes to higher education were not the sole cause of my despair in those lonely years. Arendt says human beings will always face desert conditions, and it seems reasonable to suggest that the corporatization of the university, with its overwhelmed faculty, staff, and students, can be counted among these conditions. But we have to make sure we don't adapt to desert life.[3]

How do we do that when the desert is all that we know? I worked among colleagues to whom I was not close, with the exception of a few staff members. Though I enjoyed most aspects of my work, I did not feel as though I were a part of something. My opinion was not valued; I had little say in the things that mattered in the department in which I worked. I walked to campus several days a week and sometimes spoke to no one other than a few students, and worked alone at home or in libraries or cafés the rest of the week. I would meet colleagues in the corridors on their way to a class or a meeting, and we would complain how busy we were. Beyond fatigue, I think what we really expressed was our belief in the virtue of hyper-productivity, for we took pleasure in complaining. There was a general reluctance to gather; students did not want to meet face-to-face, preferring electronic monologues to a discussion of ideas, even if monologues are conducive to misunderstandings, suspicion, or even hostility. My inbox was always full but the chairs in my office were empty. How easy it was for me to become an enemy under these conditions: an enemy of the underpaid contract instructors who wanted to take my place, of the dissatisfied customer on the one hand (the student) or the company manager on the other (the administrator), or even society in general, angry on behalf of the young whose economically promising future they wanted me to guarantee. The point hit home rather forcefully when the parents of a student I had failed due to a serious case of plagiarism complained I had ruined their child's future.

I was overcome by the weariness Camus describes, but it was not tinged by amazement when the "why" arose. He seemed not to have considered the debilitating isolation of the individual encountering her absurdity alone. There were moments when the thought that I would inhabit this bleak social terrain for years into the future filled me with a kind of low-grade panic, as though I were suffocating in the emptiness. It was desperation I felt, knowing there was no way out and no one who could help me reconcile myself to this desert. I became frantic in my attempts to build a world—I accepted teaching assignments in other departments and programs, started a discussion group with graduate students, and hosted dinner parties. But each attempt failed to relieve the intensity of my isolation and alienation. A colleague suggested the high number of faculty commuting from another city led to a desolate social environment. Others assumed the problem was living as a single woman in a neighborhood of families. Still others attributed my alienation to the kind of unusual work I do in a philosophical establishment not enamored of the unusual.

I am always tempted to say people are the same everywhere, but each group establishes a culture of shared values, norms, habits, and ways of relating within a particular territory. We could speak of national or ethnic and religious cultures, but also of workplace and even household cultures. A home, like a country, can be hospitable or inhospitable, generous or stingy, warm or cold. What is remarkable to me is that newcomers to a group tend to assimilate; human beings love to conform. The assimilation often happens rather quickly, as though we are in a hurry to feel at home again—adapting to laws and customs that might be strange to us. This may not be true when the newcomers constitute a sizable group with their own established culture and have little interest in adaptation, which explains why a sudden influx of migrants into a community can cause such fear and paranoia in the residents already living there.

Who establishes the dominant culture is a matter of historical contingencies and probably also depends on a few prominent personalities. The presence of enough people interested in maintaining pluralism is essential to maintain a humane common culture and to create a common world in which all are encouraged to participate.

The trouble is, we can get used to an inhospitable place. The desolation becomes normal, and we slip unknowingly into the belief that desolation is all there is. We forget it might be different somewhere else—in fact, we persuade ourselves that it can't possibly be better elsewhere to console ourselves in our powerlessness to change our circumstances.

IN THE DESERT

I was only able to name my place a desert—an alienating worldlessness—when I moved to another institutional home and found there a more hospitable world. Even the worst circumstances can be tolerated if we are among others who bear them with us. What was intolerable was not being a part of something, not belonging. I was not alone because I was lonely, as Lars Svendsen might insist, putting the onus on me for my pariah status; I was lonely because I had no world in which I was an active participant with others, no public realm in which my presence mattered or my voice counted.

THE IRON BAND OF TECHNOLOGY

The "iron band of terror" Arendt held responsible for the paradoxical isolation and conformity of totalitarianism's subjects has a contemporary version. We now live under the diffuse power of digital technology. The internet operates like an iron band, producing isolation while simultaneously pressing everyone into an indistinguishable mass. Social media platforms bind millions of users together, demanding conformity through political loyalties, virtue-signaling, shared indignation, and the production of identical desires. When we post or add our likes and emojis to other posts, we reinforce a particular moral or political position in a public space that no longer values pluralism and dissent; essentially, our virtual universe is a collectivized private realm where images of what we had for lunch coexist with expressions of our principled rage against injustice. Around the globe we are invited to laugh at the same memes, take selfies in the same locations, support the same political causes—or worse, hate the same groups of people and commit the same types of crimes. Those who disagree with prevailing sentiment are berated and bullied—no matter which "side" they are on—affirming the moral rectitude of those who agree.

While the internet presses us together, it also pulls us apart. Under the cloak of anonymity, raw feelings override empathic consideration or even common courtesy. A face reveals emotional nuance; without that nuance we have to rely on emojis, caps, likes, and swipes to express ourselves or refuse communication altogether. We may refuse passively in a display of deaf indifference or mute inattention, as when we use our headphones to shut out the world, but our refusal of human interaction may be more aggressive. We check our cell phones when in the company of others—an interruption equivalent to someone disrupting a private conversation—yet we no longer consider this rude. Students in lecture halls watch videos or communicate with their friends online, ignoring those who are trying to engage them in real time. They pay enormous sums of money to sit in a classroom and perform the same virtual activities they could perform elsewhere without tuition. Why are you here? I sometimes ask them, as though they are. I have seen faculty do the same at meetings and conferences; the virtual world makes us inattentive to the actual world, and we adjust our social expectations for courtesy and attention accordingly. At the more extreme end of this disengagement, we find the complete absence of anything resembling common human feeling in the virtual circulation of hate, misogyny, racism, bigotry, and images so violent that content moderators of Facebook and YouTube suffer from PTSD.[1]

When I discuss with others the negative social effects of digital technology, I am usually asked if I think it has any positive effects. Typically, the questioner reminds me that the invention of the telephone or the television—we could go as far back as the printing press—sparked a similar anxiety about the social impact of technological advancements. The implication is that we survived those developments, and we're all fine; the benefits of technology must outweigh its negative effects.

When faced with this question I am tempted to backpedal for fear of being thought a luddite—or a dinosaur, as I was called once for imposing restrictions on the use of laptops and cell phones in my classroom. But my self-doubt betrays the wishful thinking of those who believe our faith in technology is warranted; just as technology will save us from future climate catastrophe, it will save us from the harms of technology itself. We can't let this blind faith allow us to forget that now is the time for us to relearn how to live, like an athlete suddenly paralyzed by an accident or we might argue, like a terminally ill patient. Peel away our faith in technology and we find ourselves helpless in the face of the sometimes monstrous effects of human-manufactured progress.

The luddite accusation can effectively shut down the conversation, which reduces technology to an either–or issue: either we accept it for its benefits or reject it for its harms. The "techno-utopians"—as Andrew Marantz calls the "few nerdy young men" who invented the social networks in which our lives are now enmeshed—imagined they were embarking on a democratic adventure, enabling the free expression of the masses. Marantz quotes Mark Zuckerberg: "Many of us got into technology because we believe it can be a democratizing force for putting power in people's hands."[2] But the techno-utopians did not anticipate 8chan, for example, now linked to white-supremacist terrorism, or the ubiquity of online pedophilia and violent porn. Zuckerberg still claims that the world is a better place, thanks to Facebook, but he acknowledges that internet platforms can be misused. "When you connect two billion people," he admits, "you will see all the beauty and ugliness of humanity."[3]

We could have arrived at this insight without connecting two billion people, by reflecting on the history of technological advancements; like novel ideas and theoretical discoveries, new technologies are always vulnerable to abuse. Only when the negative repercussions of a particular technology are truly terrible do we lament the fact that once invented, they can't be uninvented. This is also why we might indulge a bit of self-doubt when reflecting on the social effects of technology: we love our technological inventions for the benefits they provide—we choose them, over and over again, for this reason. I am not conflicted about the fact that the internet is a force in the organization of contemporary loneliness, but since technology is a permanent feature of human life—eliciting the best and the worst from us—it demands our most thoughtful criticism.

That we do benefit from social media and digital technology more generally is obvious. When loved ones are far away, we rely on virtual modes of communication to ease the pain of missing them. Lonely, isolated, or shy individuals of all ages find relief through online communities. Studies have demonstrated the benefits of social media for children and adults with autism. Assistive technologies offer marvelous tools for the visually impaired. For the bibliophile, the researcher, and the news junkie, the internet provides abundant riches. However, as with any technological advancements, there are always trade-offs to be made, and we tend not to anticipate these in advance in order to better prepare ourselves to deal with their negative effects. If many of us are indifferent to the social effects of digital technology it is because we are devoted to productivity and efficiency, convenience, and independence. Add to this the addictive character of digital technology and the time lag between the thrill of new inventions and serious reflection on their implications, and we have a recipe for willful blindness. The charge of ludditism should not deter us from the work of criticism. The challenge is how to carry out such work when there is no way to reverse the course of technological "progress" and when we desire its riches despite its costs.

I read the critiques of our digital culture as works of mourning, odes to the social habits of another era. Franco Berardi describes the shift in the last three decades from a mechanical to a digital age as "a mutation in the texture of human experience, and in the fabric of the world itself." The mutation is constituted by the transformation of what he argues has been our dominant mode of social interaction since the Neolithic revolution. He calls this mode of relating "conjunctive," defined as a link between human beings whose source is empathy. When we conjoin, we understand another's emotions and experiences as though they were our own, and by doing so, move beyond the boundaries of our own egos to become something we were not before the interaction; conjunction leads to a meaningful exchange that engenders something new. We are transformed in the process; the exchange gives rise to new thoughts or new actions. This means a conjunctive relation is creative, since each exchange begins an "infinite number of constellations" that do not follow a preconceived pattern or design. Essential to this meaningful exchange is its context. We interpret another's meaning within a particular worldly context of bodies and things; we are attentive to our interlocutor's intention, to what is left unsaid, and to the implications of the interaction. The body is fully present in conjunctive relations, attended by sensibility and sensitivity, emotion, and empathic understanding.[4]

I hope we can all furnish examples of conjunctive ways of relating to others. In order to love someone, we must be able to move beyond the confines of our own needs and desires, and this requires empathy, vulnerability, and an openness to the unforeseeable, since we never know how a person will change us. Even in our casual interactions with others, we should notice the unpredictable quality of any encounter. One day we stop to talk to a stranger whose face and words will stay with us, sending us off along a trail of new thoughts; another day we discover something in common with a colleague we happen to meet in the hall and a new rapport begins. If we were to trace each of our lovers and friends back to their points of original contact with us, we would find these random, conjunctive encounters with a singular body in its own singular historical context.

Berardi argues the shift from a conjunctive to a "connective" method of relating to others comes with the transition to a digital age. When we connect with others, we do not understand with empathy, giving ourselves over to another's experience; rather, we understand by complying with "a syntactic structure"—with an operative grammar or code. We simply have to know the code in order to understand the message conveyed through connection and carry out what it asks of us according to precise rules of behavior and the repetition of algorithmic functions. Since there is no context surrounding the exchange, no nuances or intentions that we can actually detect, there is no ambiguity to decipher in the exchange.[5] Nothing new is created out of connection; individuals remain separate, their interaction useful but not meaningful. What remains is only a purely functional or logical linkage between bodies or machines—not logic in the service of totalitarian ideology but in the service of the efficient exchange demanded by digital capitalism.

Our social media exchanges fall into the category of Berardi's connective mode of relation. Electronic messages do not convey facial expressions or communicate body language. We have developed a code, with acronyms and emojis, to extend the limits of this communicative form, but it does not rise above the superficial. Even a profile—an attempt to disclose who we are—is written according to the rules of a code. The online dating site that promises its users will find love or sexual adventure through algorithms leaves nothing to chance. Without this chance, we merely search for a set of features or criteria we have determined in advance. The spell of the code is broken if we meet face-to-face with the person the profile attempts to summarize—a person so much more and less than the algorithms allow in the light of day.

Some may protest that conjunction is in evidence when we communicate virtually with our loved ones. I think of the affection I express in text messages and in the type of emails we might call letters. Berardi makes clear that the opposition between conjunction and connection is not a stark one, not an antithesis between two poles but a matter of "gradients, shades, and undertones."[6] At one end we would find meaningful love that alters who we are at some fundamental level, at the other, a mechanical exchange dictated by algorithms. Between these two is a wide spectrum of interactions that exhibits, to varying degrees, the sensibility of one or the other. The spectrum does not lessen the mutation we are undergoing in the very fabric of the world. We are in new territory, Berardi warns; we have to create the conceptual tools and draw the maps required to orient ourselves within it.

This distinction between conjunction and connection speaks to me as someone who lived nearly thirty years of my life before the advent of the World Wide Web and another ten before ever picking up a cell phone. When I talk to students in their early twenties, I am struck by the ineffectuality of our critiques of digital culture, given our reference points are as unfamiliar to them as my parents' reference points once were to me. I am relieved that relatives or friends with large 1960s families do not drop in on a Sunday afternoon expecting lunch, as they did when my mother was young, just as my students are relieved they don't have to spend time hunting for books in the library when writing a research essay. When I suggest to students that the communication habits we learn through social media affect our face-to-face relations, they don't understand my reference point. They do not know what our face-to-face relations were like before digital culture took over our daily lives.

Our new connective modes of exchange inevitably creep into our real-time interactions: we express rage over minor irritations, dismiss a stranger based on a look or gesture, indulge in everyday acts of rudeness with as much thought as a swipe left. The result is what we might expect: a dulling of empathy and sensitivity to nuance, of the ability to understand the complexity of another's communication. We can only recognize the simplest, most distinct categories—like black and white—never mind the confusion of shades and color combinations.

A new form of isolation appears, ironically, as the demand to communicate becomes relentless, and we want "*exit*" rather than "*access*" via the internet, as Zygmunt Bauman puts it. He believes the internet offers us a "'splendid isolation,'" since we can delete or refuse access to those we do not welcome, an isolation inconceivable in the actual world of our streets, neighborhoods, and workplaces. This is perhaps our most effective alienation from the world: rather than improving solidarity and understanding, "the Internet has facilitated practices of enclosure, separation, exclusion, enmity and strife," and these practices now infiltrate our offline interactions.[7] We choose this isolation, no longer socially obligated to listen or attend to someone we don't consider important or interesting. We don't have to listen to the opinions of those who disagree with us, either; in fact, disagreement is experienced as offensive by the progressive-minded individual, avoided for fear of hurting others or being hurt by them.

Are we at risk of forgetting the meaning of solidarity, community, and perhaps even friendship, as we adjust to the isolation of connectivity? A student recently confessed to me in a conversation after class: I don't know what a friend is. I was taken aback by her admission, not of being without friends, which would be terrible enough, but of having no understanding of the concept. Looking into this young woman's inscrutable face, I wondered how many of her peers would admit the same at a time in their lives when friends should be the core of their daily existence.

There are obvious differences between the iron band of terror in Arendt's discussion of totalitarianism and the iron band of technology in my formulation. While fear forced individuals to submit to the iron band of terror, the promise of pleasure and the fulfilment of desire invite us to submit to the iron band of technology. In fact, we willingly relinquish our privacy and individuality for the narcissistic feed the internet offers us, the permission to exclude those who disagree with us or simply irritate us, the flow of information, and for the convenience of online shopping. Loneliness is the price we pay for these pleasures and conveniences— essentially, for the luxury of nobody bothering us in real time.[8]

Technology tries to compensate by mitigating the loneliness it causes; it takes with one hand and gives back with the other and soon we forget the original theft in our gratitude for the compensatory gift. In this respect the rule of technology is unlike that of twentieth-century totalitarianism, which did not benefit anyone except those who wielded it as an instrument of terror. But what kind of sociality is returned to us? It is no coincidence that the less we experience a sense of home among those bodies we happen to live among and the less we experience care, conviviality, and solidarity in what we may surely call our own dark times, the more appealing we find the rigid identities the internet offers us. We should not be surprised, Berardi says, that the longing to belong when there is nothing to belong to leads to a "nostalgic desire for an identity that never really existed in the first place," and this might be the starting point for identity-based violence.[9]

Just as it is reductive to blame the lonely for their loneliness, it is reductive to attribute contemporary loneliness solely to the connective mode of relating engendered by technology. The mutation we are undergoing—"in the texture of human experience, and in the fabric of the world"—takes place in the wider context of what Berardi calls "capitalist absolutism," whose destructive effects are visible in the environment, economy, education, social welfare, and in the impotence of social movements to reverse these effects. What resistance is possible when solidarity has been compromised, the consequence of increasing competition and productivity, and "an endless intensification of the rhythms of work"? Without solidarity we are left in a desert of loneliness and despair that is difficult to resist.[10]

So we bring in the government to launch a loneliness strategy headed by a Minister of Loneliness or a national campaign led by civil society organizations to churn out reports on how to build community infrastructure and empower social connections, and we get busy instituting Men's Sheds, bereavement groups, community cafés, "relationships education" for youth, singles clubs, and "Rent-a-Family" services.[11] And we turn to the loneliness experts for their toolkit solutions: join a swim team, a volunteer organization, or a pottery class; try "social fitness exercises" that will force you to look up from your phone; buy a loneliness app that will remind you to smile more; or implement a sharing hour at your workplace. Let's not forget the pundits' platitude that loneliness is as harmful as smoking cigarettes; it is costing employers through missed work, increased staff turnover, and lowered productivity, and draining our healthcare systems. Loneliness undermines the smooth functioning of capitalist absolutism and exposes the mythical proportions of its promise of happiness.

Maybe some of us will benefit from generic anti-loneliness regimens. But these solutions appear absurdly ineffectual when we consider that organized loneliness makes it difficult to distinguish between loneliness and any of its accompaniments: isolation, depression, mental illness, anxiety, boredom, stress, frustration, and panic—or worse, violence.

If loneliness is the price we pay for the freedom of nobody bothering us, it follows that to resist organized loneliness we must accept inconvenience and allow ourselves to be bothered by others. This means that solidarity, friendship, courtesy, and care, no longer taken for granted, will become forms of resistance against reconciling ourselves to life in a social desert. For this struggle we need a "life-giving" source like love and friendship, an oasis without which "we would not know how to breathe."[12]

SOCIAL FAILURE

There is considerable alarm in Japan over lonely deaths, or *kodokushi*. The elderly and the sick are dying alone, sometimes undiscovered for weeks, months, or occasionally even years. The dead may have had children who failed to visit, friends who moved away, or neighbors who remained strangers. When the bodies are eventually found, cleaning companies arrive to clear out the maggots and make the apartment habitable again. In one estimate, there are some 30,000 such deaths in Japan each year.[1]

But lonely deaths are not exclusive to the elderly. In the summer of 2019 the body of Mason Pendrous, a first-year student at Canterbury University in New Zealand, was found in his campus residence room a month or more after he died. One line in a news report stands out for me: "The dead boy's room was at the end of a long corridor and not attended to by the hall's cleaners, who worked only on common areas." The line reads as though the writer is looking for a reasonable explanation of how a person could die and remain undiscovered for weeks on end, as though it is more surprising to know that campus residence cleaners do not enter every room than to know that a person could live there without ever being noticed by those living down the hall.[2]

These deaths are deeply disturbing. How have we arrived at this point: a person lives and dies without being sufficiently close to anyone, so fundamentally alone that no one notices the lack of movement in a neighboring apartment, an overflowing mailbox in the lobby, a door that stopped opening and closing? Arendt says when we lose our worldly bearings, we are left in a barren landscape without others on whom to rely. When everything between us has withered away, the desert spreads. The evidence is all around us: rising rates of suicide, depression, anxiety, and self-harm, especially among youth—even children—and lonely deaths.

Many try to adapt; those who find adjustment impossible will wonder what is wrong with them. But the inability to reconcile ourselves to desert life, Arendt reminds us, is precisely what proves we are still human.[3]

Maladjustment can be quiet and private as frustration and disillusionment over a lonely, meaningless existence are turned inward. Consider the new version of recluses appearing in wealthy, technologically advanced countries, first noted in Japan in the 1990s where the phenomenon as well as those who experience it are called *hikikomori*—literally "pulling in." Hikikomori withdraw completely from society, isolating themselves in their rooms for months, years, or even decades, most of them financially supported by their parents. Numbers are difficult to estimate, but it is assumed there are hundreds of thousands of hikikomori in Japan and by some estimates even a million or more.[4] The majority of these are men, and while youth and young adults have been the focus of studies until recently, the rise of middle-aged hikikomori is gaining attention.[5]

Though routines and behaviors vary more than the public discourse about them conveys, the common narrative is that hikikomori stop going to school or work, refuse to eat or communicate with their families, and lock themselves into a bedroom which they may leave only at night to buy food. Their contact with the world is limited, for the most part, to the virtual. Older hikikomori often began their social withdrawal at retirement; in a recent survey, one in three in this category was financially supported by the savings or pensions of aging parents. In the many personal accounts that are surfacing, hikikomori express shame, a sense of failure, and unremitting loneliness. Karin Amamiya, one of the most outspoken advocates for disaffected Japanese youth, describes the "existential angst" of hikikomori as "ontological insecurity." This is a reference to the lack of recognition and sense of belonging experienced among those most negatively affected by Japan's ruthless deregulation of labor beginning in the 1990s. "Everyone needs a place, identity, affiliation," Amamiya insists, "an *ibasho* [home] that finds us necessary."[6] But the shift from secure, salaried employment to precarious, flexible, and temporary work, and the corresponding dehumanization of "disposable" workers, means these needs are unmet.

Debate continues as to whether hikikomori is a pathology in need of psychiatric intervention or an appropriate response to the absence of meaningful employment and close relationships in a country in which it is a challenge to establish them, and in which a successful career and traditional family are still the markers of success (though increasingly difficult to achieve owing to job precarity and women's declining interest in marriage and motherhood).[7] As a proponent of the second view, Franco Berardi says social withdrawal is actually a healthy response to the "unbearable stress of competition, mental exploitation, and precarity. . . . A fully understandable withdrawal from hell."[8] Unable to survive a hostile world, hikikomori are "refugees from one kind of ordinary," as Anne Allison puts it; they live as though in exile.[9]

The catalyst for intensified public interest in social withdrawal as a national problem in Japan was several high-profile killings and a case of kidnapping by perpetrators considered to be hikikomori in the year 2000.[10] Not every refusal to adapt to the loss of worldly bearings—conscious or unconscious—is quiet or private, nor does maladjustment necessarily provide evidence that humanity prevails. We are hearing the phrase "lone killer" or "lone wolf" applied to the men responsible for a rising number of mass murders in recent decades in the United States especially, but also in Canada, France, Norway, Japan, and elsewhere.[11] We might speculate on what is new in these solo acts of terror and what their perpetrators tend to have in common: a history of isolation and loneliness, heavy internet use, economic privilege, deep grievances against women, Muslims, or other groups, and a desire for violent revenge.

Elliot Rodger is probably the most well known of these perpetrators. Before killing six young people and injuring fourteen others near the University of California, Santa Barbara, in May 2014, at the age of twenty-two, Rodger sent a manifesto to his family and his therapist. It is a lengthy chronicle of loneliness going back to his childhood that reveals a deeply disturbed young man, insecure about his height and physical "weakness," his mixed-race heritage, his virginity, and his inability to fit in with the "cool" kids at school, despite all the stylish clothes and video games his parents gave him. He also expresses the grandiose fantasies and lack of empathy typical of psychopaths, and testifies to a torturous, unfulfilled sexual desire for women that is deeply misogynist. This hatred motivated his ultimate goal: to punish women for rejecting him, along with anyone who enjoyed the pleasures of sex that he was denied.[12]

Rodger is now known as the patron saint of the Incel movement—the "involuntarily celibate"—an online subculture that draws lonely men into a virtual community of other men who have been unable to form the romantic attachments to women they feel are owed to them. Rodger influenced the mass killings carried out in Toronto by Alek Minassian, in Tallahassee, Florida, by Scott Paul Beierle, and in a Parkland, Florida, high school by Nikolas Cruz—all in 2018. Their extreme misogyny is matched by Anders Breivik's and Brenton Tarrant's hatred of Muslims, and Dylann Roof's anti-Black racism.

Frieda Fromm-Reichmann's question with respect to her schizophrenic patients is appropriate to ask here: "What has gone wrong in the history of the lonely ones?" In the case of the lone killer, it is probably impossible to separate a history of loneliness from mental disturbance, narcissism, a profound sense of failure, and a meaningless existence. The relation of these to misogyny or racism constitutes a study on its own. George Sodini, who opened fire at a fitness center in a suburb of Pittsburgh in August 2009, killing three women and wounding nine, apparently didn't exhibit any signs of mental illness or psychopathy and had no criminal record. He left a diary that narrated the nine months before he carried out his revenge against all the women who didn't save him from the disappointment of his life. The isolation he describes is total—for thirty years he had not made a close friend or been able to work toward the achievement of any goal. He wrote that there was even less in his future than in his empty present. Sodini's life was meaningless apart from his plan to kill women he didn't know who were participating in an aerobics class.[13]

The terror caused by the lonely, armed man, superfluous and enraged, bereft of a world beyond the virtual, is vastly different from the terror of twentieth-century totalitarianism that gave Arendt the impetus to write of organized loneliness. But here too, in the unthinkable actions of the lone killer, we find isolation as a fertile ground for terror. We can't know if Rodger and Sodini, or the perpetrators of similar crimes, would have carried out mass murder had they not been lonely and isolated, with easy access to guns and internet attention. The issue is more complex. But I think we can conclude the prevalence of this kind of terror is a symptom of contemporary social failure. We have arrived at the extreme end of the inextricably related psychological, social, and political effects of a ravaged world.

These are all lonely deaths—the unremembered and unaccounted for body, the socially dead "refugee" in exile, and the lone killer whose death to the world of others has already occurred long before he takes the lives of his victims. In different ways they stand as testaments to what we need and to what we are missing.

PART III
WHAT DO WE NEED?

PANDEMIC PAUSE

As I write, most of the global population is at various stages of lockdown due to the Covid-19 pandemic. In my city of over six million, we are entering week eight of a mandate to "shelter in place." The world is on pause and to say the effects are extraordinary seems a vast understatement. No one yet knows the degree of economic damage that will follow or the extent of the suffering caused by millions of people losing their livelihoods overnight. For many, hunger is more of a threat than the virus; they risk their lives going to work and they risk their lives staying home. We await the political fallout with baited breath—will the pandemic feed populism or starve it? We already know how quickly authoritarian leaders profit from an increase in the power to control their populations, and how quickly fear and panic render us passive. A pandemic is a golden opportunity to institute (even to legislate) the isolation that keeps us obedient and immobilized by our collective panic. But I am more interested here in what an abrupt cessation of social life tells us about what we need, since deprivation exposes the difference between luxury and necessity.

A city is an eerie place without public life. Judging by the recent glut of photographs in the media depicting empty city squares and streets throughout the world, each one interrupted only by a requisite lone figure, we seem fascinated by the absence of visible signs of life. Perhaps we identify with that figure and experience the horror of being the sole survivor of catastrophe. We can hear the silence, feel its barren loneliness. Maybe the absence is only a reminder of the nothingness of death; we search the image for meaning, trying to comprehend what will always remain incomprehensible.

I forego long walks, since there is no public destination—a friend's house, a library, or a café. When I do venture out, I think of Jane Jacobs, whose indignation over thoughtless urban planning produced brilliant discussions of what makes a city a dynamic living environment—sidewalk life and its public characters, and spaces for children's play and the mingling of strangers or neighbors. Now I walk through what feels like a dystopian film set. In the park near my house, only beginning to turn green at the close of a cold April, there are solitary actors on their separate stages: to my left, a teenager shoots hoops at one end of the basketball court, while at the other end a woman talks animatedly on a cell phone, her arms flailing in the air. On my right, a middle-aged man, possibly homeless, sits alone on a bench staring vacantly at the patch of grass in front of him. He does not look up when I pass by though I am already smiling at him in acknowledgment. Beyond him a woman grips her toddler's arm and explains, wearily, why he can't climb on the play structure. Wariness permeates the air around all of us. We are enclosed in our own separate worlds, as disconnected as the subjects in an Edward Hopper painting.

The wariness is paradoxically paired with a new sense of solidarity. We inhabit a city known for polite reserve and apologetic deference; suspicion unnerves us even if it is a reasonable response to a disease that can be transmitted before the onset of symptoms. The first day social distancing was implemented at my local grocery store, the piped music was inexplicably shut off, as though management worried sound might spread the virus or playing music might be considered insensitive during so serious a time. Now, months later, customers give one another a wide berth and avoid eye contact; this too seems absurd, since no one is infected by a glance. I suspect the guardedness is not actually new but only more noticeable now that we feel a sudden solidarity with strangers. Toronto is a city in which meeting the gaze of those we pass by on the street is uncomfortable at the best of times. It isn't unfriendliness exactly but a social habit of cool reserve the origins of which are unclear; it may be the pretentions of the professional and business classes who believe this to be the proper attitude for a worldly city, or it may be the weather.

In the grocery store the contradiction between wariness and solidarity is evident; there is a palpable sense of both fear and compassion. On one visit, an elderly man reprimands me for touching a carton of tomatoes I decide not to buy, accusing me of having no human decency.

Despite my best attempts to avoid him, we encounter each other again at the fish counter and this time he tells me loudly to "Get lost!" Some customers bestow sympathetic, masked smiles on one other. In the wider world, we hear of exceptional acts of kindness—even the sacrifice of life—occurring side by side with acts of greed and hostility, racism, and domestic violence. A crisis brings out the best and the worst of human behavior. Doctors and nurses are dying in their efforts to save the lives of their severely ill patients, while others pull out guns when forced to wear a mask while shopping. Volunteers throughout the world distribute food or telephone the lonely, while individuals and companies are busy profiting from human pain. I could go on.

I stand at the picture window in the front of my house to look for signs of life, tempted to wave at passing cyclists or pedestrians because suddenly every human interaction carries a weight it did not previously carry. If neighbors appear, I step outside to chat from my porch, savoring the brief exchanges we once took for granted or even considered irritating interruptions of work or rest at the end of the day. Did we understand, before the pandemic, how meaningful these mundane encounters are, scattered across an ordinary day? Did we appreciate the beauty of a facial expression and a body's gestures that attest to everything we share—a myriad of sensuous and emotional responses to the world around us, all infinitely variable yet common to each other? I miss the affection of my dearest friends, taking in the complicated movements of their eyes and mouths and hands as we sink into the depths of a conversation that pulls us into the world we have created between us. I also miss greeting the owners of my neighborhood produce store and complaining about the weather or the housing market while I select the best lettuce and zucchini. Did we know, before now, how greedy our senses are?

The pause we are experiencing is a suspension not only of these social interactions but of business as usual. The daily operations of technocapitalism are breaking down like a noisy machine that smokes and sputters until it grinds to a halt. The air clears and our senses stir as though waking up from a drug-induced sleep. In the early days of the lockdowns we heard the encouraging news that in Venice the canals had cleared enough to see fish in their depths, while the residents of Punjab could view the Himalayan range for the first time in decades. If it were not for the economic deprivation and loneliness many are suffering, we would feel as Sisyphus did coming down the mountain with a light, exuberant step, released from his burden long enough to take pleasure in his surroundings.

In the early weeks of the lockdown, those of us who were protected from the worst fallout may have been relieved by the sudden solitude and respite. Events, meetings, travel, and conferences were cancelled, deadlines extended, and the morning and evening commutes ceased to take their daily mental toll. The frantic movement of the city slowed almost overnight and suddenly felt unnecessary. What were we doing that made us so busy? Did we have to be forced to recognize the pace we kept was unsustainable? I reveled in the change for a brief week or two, despite the fear of contagion and an uncertain future, and caught my breath for the first time after months of the usual work pressures. People enjoyed more time with their children, neighbors, and the old friends who reappeared in their lives, and a sudden pleasure in the new solitude. Those of us old enough to remember waxed nostalgic about the 1990s or earlier, when it was normal for kids to play in the streets after school or neighbors to congregate outdoors. That old sense of a neighborhood has returned, as we spill out of our private spaces of confinement to interact with others. A friend called me recently and I realized it was the first time in years that anyone besides a phone solicitor had called without first arranging a time. Suddenly, in the face of an existential threat, the work that drives us seems less important than talking to our friends.

Then the zoom meetings began to interrupt the pause and, for me, a flurry of policy changes, emergency measures, and panicked messages from students. The sudden shift to working in a virtual space is an opportune moment to increase management and surveillance, and to eliminate individuality. Governments around the world are ignoring the advice of their experts as they race to open the economy—and most are on board with this rush since everyone needs a job to survive. The brilliance of technocapitalism is that it always regroups after an attack, very like a virus that mutates, frustrating the best attempts of medicine and science to control it.

The order to stay home has made us even more reliant on technology to communicate with others and to work from home if we are able to do so. Even those of us most critical of social media's effects (or least fluent in its dialects and mechanics) appreciate what it offers us now in our seclusion. But many find the virtual less than satisfying, reinforcing those arguments made before the pandemic—what seems a lifetime ago—that we need our social media platforms only as supplements to our face-to-face time with others, or we need them because they are better than having no social life at all. Despite technotopian dreams of a brave new virtual world, has anyone really imagined what it would be like to be completely dependent on the internet for human interaction? It may surprise some of us to discover we need a sensuous world like we need clean air to breathe.

How else do we explain the sudden comeback of the telephone conversation? One of the largest telecommunications companies in the United States has reported that the number of daily wireless calls on weekdays is more than double the number of calls made on Mother's Day, which is historically one of the busiest days of the year for phone calls.[1] The length of the calls has also increased. Though everyone was prepared for more internet use, this return to an antiquated technology is a surprise. But it shouldn't be. The technologies that allow us to see one another feel too mediated given that our eyes do not meet directly, our voices are not as clear, and the connection is more likely to malfunction. We may not actually have more time to talk on the phone with our friends, but we have more of a need to do so.

For all the hype about online learning in recent decades, North American students are balking at the prospect of online classes in the upcoming academic year. They protest they will not get the educational experience they paid for if classrooms are virtual.[2] Masha Gessen goes so far as to say the myth of college education in America has been "shattered" by the coronavirus, and it is not only because the bright future colleges promise their graduates is now an uncertain and perhaps terrifying one. "Life has been drained of content and the plot is lost," she writes after listening to a student complain that "online classes are boring."[3] With no place for bodies to gather, no common experience of cramped classrooms, tasteless dining hall fare, eccentric professors, or the excitement of new ideas, the students lose focus and incentive. I can't imagine this loss myself, as I recall with nostalgia all the lunch hours in cafeterias talking about what happened in class or the late nights spent in libraries to cram for exams with my friends. There is always a social element to learning. It occurs as often in the hallways, dining rooms, and student residences as in the classroom.

Many of us may want to return to work to escape a private existence that begins to feel suffocating. Financial need is not the only motivation for leaving the house; to one extent or another, we also need and desire a public life. My own work habits are relatively unchanged, since I often worked at home before the pandemic rendered us all housebound. Those of us who spend our days with books and ideas, or tools of a creative occupation, are perhaps specially equipped for an injunction to stay at home. But our work keeps us in relation to a world of others; we don't write books for no one to read, a piece of music to remain unheard, or create a work of art to be hidden away. If I spend my day reading, I am very much in the world—in conversation with other thinkers whose own worlds either parallel or contrast mine. But I miss the flow of human life on city streets, with its random encounters and events—even the crush of people on the subway at rush hour—because it furnishes my day with experiences to mull over and discuss with friends or students. Without this flow there is still the rich experience of an interior life, but it begins to lose focus and vitality, like the world of a landscape painter who is forced to rely on the memory of rivers and mountain peaks in their absence.

It seems a terrible question to ask, but at what point do we decide that some forms of suffering are worse than death, as the bedridden patient must decide when her pain has become intolerable? If we learn anything from our current pandemic, it is that exclusively inhabiting a private realm is as dangerous to human life as exclusively inhabiting a public realm. Either way, we are deprived of something vital—a need to appear in the world and a need to hide from it, as Arendt would say. For those who live alone, the order to stay home may come close to replicating the conditions of solitary confinement, which we know can lead to depression and madness. I am witness to the despair of my young adult son who is paralyzed by the loss of daily interactions with others, unable even to engage in the creative projects that normally sustain him. He suffocates in the emptiness of his days, trapped in a self he is paradoxically losing.

For those who live with spouses, family members, or friends in close quarters, a home could become the hell in Sartre's play, *No Exit*. How can we be surprised by the rise in domestic violence? Couples, or parents and their children, are forced to constitute their own public, magnifying the social exclusivity already the norm. The household becomes a territory with closed borders, ruled democratically or tyrannically, that mimics the inequality, greed, or violence that comes with any territory. Hopefully, also the companionship—yet friendship and love, too, can suffocate when closed to the world. The pandemic certainly proves we need more than one or two others to fill out our lives.

Supporting the economy is not the only reason everyone is eager for lockdowns to end. In any human crisis suffering becomes bearable— even meaningful—when we share its burden with others; what makes it unbearable is to carry it alone. Isolation is unsustainable; it drains life of all meaningful content. Yet we are being told that until a vaccine is produced[4] this will be our new normal, governed by mandates to stay six feet away from another body, shun handshakes and hugs, and cover the part of our faces most essential for putting others at ease. What will this new normal do to us if it lasts a year or longer? We say we will remember the revelations of this interregnum, the sudden appreciation of the workers who saved us—from healthcare professionals to grocery store cashiers—and the new respect for solitude as well as friendly neighbors. But interregnums end; the pull of the status quo tends to be more powerful than the will to imagine something new.

At least now we know what we need.

TO BELONG

The poet A. K. Ramanujan noted in his diary on November 9, 1979, the "appalling" feeling that at the age of fifty he was "quite an amateur" thinker and writer. He decided he was experiencing his first fear of aging, "of being unexpressed, of having missed the boat, therefore of not belonging and so of not wanting to belong."[1] I am curious about the turn of phrase at the end of this line. Did he not want to belong because he feared he didn't belong anyway? Or is there a *not wanting* to belong in the very *wanting* to belong itself? And what was he pining to belong/not belong to?

How well I understand the contradiction of wanting and not wanting to belong—sometimes feeling lonely when I am not part of a group and sometimes feeling hemmed in when I am. I attribute this ambivalence to having once belonged to a collective with bonds so powerful my autonomy was at risk. But maybe I was simply born with an independent spirit, and belonging will remain equally attractive and repulsive to me. There is a dialectical movement in belonging between proximity and distance, or togetherness and separation, that can't—and I think shouldn't—be resolved. The trouble is, proximity can be irresistible—we don't want to "miss the boat" and be left behind. I think Ramanujan is right to note this worry accompanies middle age, when we sense for the first time that the world will go on without us.

The value of belonging is something we tend to take for granted, as we do the value of community—the social form that most often captures that to which we want to belong. My ambivalence toward both belonging and community does not prevent me from insisting we do need to belong in both our public and private worlds. My concern is that we have simplified the meaning of belonging, and this may have something to do with our reductive understanding of community. The emphasis on membership in an identity category as the object of belonging—an emphasis that has intensified over the last three decades—has distorted what it means to belong. We have lost the other side of the contradiction expressed so enigmatically by Ramanujan—the sense of "not wanting to belong," which immediately releases us from a belonging that constrains us.

To consider what we mean when we say we belong, I note two distinct but related definitions in the *Merriam-Webster* dictionary: to belong means to be "attached" or "bound"—by birth, for example—and also to be an "attribute" or "part" of a person or thing. These definitions work together: when we belong, we are bound to a place or group of people, and this attachment indicates we are part of something beyond ourselves. There are both private and public versions of belonging. We belong to the persons we love, to whom we are deeply attached, and we belong to a workplace, neighborhood, or country, in which we feel part of a world. Within these places we are bound to the things that color our surroundings; when we belong to a neighborhood, our feelings of attachment or being a part of something arise through the familiarity of the trees along our streets or in our gardens, our neighbors, and the mountains, lakes, or skyscrapers near us. Missing from *Merriam-Webster*'s definition is sentiment; to belong is to *feel* we belong, perhaps best expressed by the feeling of being *at home*.

To understand this feeling, we can look to the obvious examples of not-belonging. A refugee who has lost a home, community, work, and friends seems not to belong anywhere. A homeless person might feel she doesn't have a part in society, though she may be attached to a particular street and her possessions, however meager. Hikikomori have been described as "homeless at home," feeling superfluous and disconnected from the world.[2] Lonely persons, members of ethnic or sexual minorities, the retired or unemployed, those suffering from disease or mental illness—all may experience a lack of attachment or the feeling of not being an essential part of something.

The danger of not-belonging is pointed out by Arendt, for whom belonging is a core human need since all rights—even the right to have rights—are tied to belonging to a homeland. It is the refugee who best highlights this need. Deprived of rights because she has left the territory to which she belongs by birth, she is at the same time deprived of "a place in the world which makes opinions significant and actions effective."[3] To have a place, and thus the opportunity to participate in making a world, is even more fundamental for Arendt than citizens' rights to freedom and justice, since without such a place no one would have the right to have these rights.[4] The danger of not-belonging is the danger of worldlessness—the stateless lose citizenship and profession, but also opinions valued by others and actions by which to "identify" and "specify" themselves.[5] Without the capacity to express ourselves and carry out actions in a common world, we lose what is unique about each of us.[6]

We can stretch this further than our attachment to a homeland that legitimates our right to have rights. We need to belong in the same way to workplaces that value our contributions and to any variation of organized, collective life. To belong in this sense has little to do with one's ethnic, religious, or sexual identity, to mention only three of a long list of categories to which we might say we belong. What matters for Arendt is place and what we do within this place to ensure it remains habitable for future generations.

When I consider belonging from the perspective of place, I feel less ambivalent. To feel at home simply means we are comfortable within familiar surroundings and with those who share it with us—we are part of the furniture, so to speak. It does not mean we are forced to conform in our thinking or behavior, because our individual opinions are valued. Nor does it mean we belong only because we can display the proper identity card. We can feel at home without sacrificing the distance between us, the mark of our individuality and freedom. If we are asked to sacrifice this distance, we are no longer a part of something since there is nothing to individuate us from one another.

PROXIMITY

My cat follows me silently whenever I leave my desk to work in another room. She finds the closest spot, settles down on my papers or on my lap as I write, and feigns sleep. She bides her time, knowing I will get up to make tea, at which point she will claim my chair, the cushioned surface that bears the scent and impression of my body. My cat knows the pleasure of proximity.

The first time I lived alone for longer than a few months, I occupied what we call a single-family dwelling on a street with similar single-family dwellings, each one inhabited by a single family in a neighborhood with more of the same. I experienced a distinct desire for proximity, a need not precisely for love or affection (though proximity and love often go together) but for a physical nearness to others. When we live close to others, we take for granted the comfort of human sounds in another room—someone steps across the floor above us, runs a shower, hums a tune, or types on a keyboard. In an apartment building we might hear children down the hall, laughter in neighboring living rooms, or the noise of televisions and video games. The pleasure of proximity is expressed by the protagonist of Jenny Erpenbeck's novel *Go, Went, Gone*, a retired Classics professor who lives alone after the death of his wife. While listening to a friend play the piano in his house one afternoon, Richard ruminates on *"the joy of the parallel universe."* He realizes how long he has lived without the sounds of another person in his daily life and recalls how content he had been when working at his desk while his wife practiced the viola in the next room.[1]

At that time and place in my life, I found living alone nearly unbearable. I did not know which contributing factor was the most important: my alienating work environment, living an hour's drive away from my closest friends and my son, being single in a neighborhood of couples and families, or the fact that I could not hear anyone on the other side of the walls of my house. The silent space I normally crave after a full day of interacting with others became oppressive after a few days. The objects that surrounded me—my books, plants, art, and photographs—offered no consolation; in fact, I felt some pity for them since they inhabited a space defined by silence. I knew I needed to take a break from my work, but whenever I did, I wandered from room to room not knowing what to do with myself. I thought of places I could go, but when I considered the enjoyment of visiting them would come from sharing observations and reflections about anything trivial or significant that might happen along the way, there was little incentive. I felt as though I lived under house arrest, my body imprisoned by the sheer, empty space around it.

The literature on loneliness often neglects our need for the simple presence of other bodies. We naturally take the body into account when we reflect on sexual intimacy, but not when we think about less intense experiences of human intimacy; we ignore the wide spectrum of embodied encounters between friends, acquaintances, or even strangers: handshakes, eye contact, sympathetic smiles, a touch on the arm, or a pat on the back. We are drawn into nearness, like the "clinamen" Lucretius discovered—his term for the swerve of atoms toward one another—or like bees who orient themselves to the colony by releasing pheromones. We congregate in cities, not only for jobs but to live among a greater diversity of people; we bring our laptops to cafés to work or study to escape being alone at home; we flock to parks in the midst of a global pandemic, risking our health in order to be near others. Human empathy is maximized by this proximity of bodies (though empathy can also be minimized by proximity)—and another's struggle becomes my own. As I write, an unprecedented groundswell of protest against racism has erupted in cities around the world, the immediate catalyst yet another Black person's death at the hands of an American police officer. This global solidarity is one of the more inspiring effects of proximity.

I found immediate relief from the loneliness of my silent home when I moved into an apartment in a house with other tenants, located in a more cosmopolitan city. The sound of life on the other side of the walls provided some reassurance that I was part of a greater human collectivity. In urban density I experienced the comfort of an abundance of people just beyond my doorstep. I joined in the mayhem of moving life forms and felt less alone, like Vivian Gornick, who writes of sitting down to dinner by herself in her New York City apartment, comforted by the life outside her windows. "My mind flashes on all who crossed my path today," she explains. "I hear their voices, I see their gestures, I start filling in lives for them. Soon they are company, great company."[2]

DISTANCE

We know that proximity is not always pleasurable, since partners or neighbors get angry and children irritable, and peaceful protests turn violent and destructive. Too much nearness can inspire the opposite desire—for distance.

Distance means I am separate from you; my needs are not necessarily the same as yours. It means I have my own will that pushes me to act this way or that, in one direction or another, and there is no one else to blame for which direction I take since I am solely responsible for my decisions and actions. It means I may want something you do not, feel something you do not, and I have the capacity to think for myself. The distance between us means I am an individual; there is something singular in my existence that is not replicated in you. This singularity implies freedom—it is because I am irreplaceable by you that I know the way I choose to live is up to me.[1]

My singularity needs to be protected, as does yours—the distance between us is an existential need. This may sound decadent at a time when the individual appears to need less defending than the collective. In fact, a pronounced focus on the self is intensifying a range of antisocial sentiment and behavior in our actual and virtual worlds, from indifference to hate and passive aggression to violence. An inflated sense of individualism is a basic feature of our technocapitalist present, aptly captured in the Canadian Conservative Party's campaign slogan during the 2019 federal election: "Time for you to get ahead." Ahead of whom is too obvious a question—the implication is *everyone*. We are witnessing a particularly insidious effect of this self-centeredness—the uncontrolled spread of a virus due to the unwillingness of some people to help protect others from a terrible disease and possible death, a refusal justified on the basis of individual freedom.

How do we protect distance without promoting an exaggerated individualism and narcissistic sense of freedom? Human beings have always struggled for individual autonomy when threatened by the overreach of a collective, at least when we have had the capacity to struggle. We have fought against arranged marriages, the belief we should stay with an abusive partner, parental authority to dictate our educational interests and pursuits, and the law's power to force us to have children or the government's to decide how many we should have. Entire populations have fought for collective autonomy from an authoritative state. Even those we might assume are unhappy with independence—the elderly, the disabled, or singles—may, in fact, willingly accept the trade-offs, including loneliness, for the freedom of a little distance. As the American surgeon and writer Atul Gawande points out in *Being Mortal*, a clear historical pattern tells us we will choose independence if we have the opportunity and ability to do so. The context of this claim is the story of his grandfather—supported in his elderly years in India by an enormous extended family whose role it was to ensure he could "continue to live as he desired," regardless of the family's sacrifices and intergenerational conflict.[2] We think this traditional old age is what we want, Gawande says, but it is only nostalgia.[3] Human beings have a basic need for independence, though they don't always have the means to grasp it.

Distance and proximity are always in tension. The individual must constantly resist being swallowed up by the crowd or subdued by forces outside of her control. Georg Simmel's early twentieth-century analysis of the individual in relation to society captures the tension well: "The deepest problems of modern life flow from the attempt of the individual to maintain the independence and individuality of his existence against the sovereign powers of society."[4] The "society" is variable. Simmel compares individuality in the small town or community to that in the big city. The smaller the social unit, the stronger its sovereign powers and the weaker the strength of its individuals to resist the demand for conformity. Distance is hard to protect in a small town. In larger social units, on the other hand, the sovereign powers and therefore social unity are weaker, allowing individuals greater autonomy to be who they want to be, develop their own lifestyles, and make their own choices.[5] Quite simply, if there were nothing to call individual, there would be nothing unique about us; not only would power be given free rein to determine and subordinate us, life would be boring. To be a member of society, to belong to anyone or anything, one must be an individual.

I must point out that Simmel was writing a century before anyone was shouting about the right to protect oneself with a gun or the right to refuse to protect others during a pandemic by wearing a mask. These protestations are not made out of respect for anyone's freedom, nor out of a need for individuality or distance, since both freedom and distance are meaningless outside of a world of others. Simone de Beauvoir puts it best when she declares: "I am oppressed if I am thrown into prison, but not if I am kept from throwing my neighbor into prison."[6] My freedom assumes yours. I can and should be stopped from doing something that destroys your freedom, or neither of us is free.

Distance is meaningless without proximity. Each term must reflect the other. Roland Barthes expresses this evocatively when he suggests distance is a value but one "that won't destroy affect"—distance is "irrigated by tender feeling" and respect.[7] He is assuming the collective world de Beauvoir assumes. Distance does not need to imply the dissolution of collective experience.

I would still like to know whether we can be individuals—grasping what freedom is to be had in what distance is ours—without paying the price of loneliness. For this we need those indispensable public relationships that fall somewhere along the spectrum between intimate friends and strangers.

IN THE NEIGHBORHOOD

The injunction to stay at home in order to contain the spread of Covid-19 seems to have revived an old-fashioned sense of neighborhood in urban centers where those in our immediate surroundings are not normally a source of social life. Neighbors gather on front yards and driveways to chat at an appropriate distance, and children race by on their bicycles or play on the now deserted streets. Now we know what it takes to appreciate the unique social form a neighborhood offers: a daily life trapped in the private realm and limited to disembodied interactions in the virtual sphere. Location suddenly matters—we can't meet colleagues at work or visit friends on the other side of the city, so we interact more with those nearby.

I will call a neighborhood a community of chance, since it is based solely on the contingent circumstance of where we happen to live at any point in time. Our belonging to a neighborhood is not typically based on a specific identity, as is often the case for membership in a community (though neighborhoods can certainly become uniform and exclusive), and we do not usually get to choose our neighbors. We occupy a place in a neighborhood simply because we are born there or at some point move in. If we stay there long enough, we may find ourselves an integral part of its fabric.

How a neighborhood comes to have a fabric is due to a number of social practices, probably common to cities around the world, despite some cultural specificities. These practices are the focus of *The Death and Life of Great American Cities*, the work Jane Jacobs calls her "attack" on the city planning in fashion during the late 1950s. Jacobs illuminates the social conditions necessary to sustain the diversity and vibrancy of cities, and details how these conditions are cultivated—in a neighborhood, for example, where numerous casual, seemingly trivial, public encounters turn out to be vital for the life of its inhabitants. I doubt the social conditions for a neighborhood have changed much in the sixty years since, though they are more difficult to foster.

Every urban neighborhood has what Jacobs calls "sidewalk life." A sidewalk constitutes the public space in which we are most likely to meet those who live near us as we walk to work, go shopping, accompany children to school, and take dogs to the park. The rapport we build with strangers and acquaintances on the sidewalk remains casual, emblematic of the distance a public space provides. Jacobs is always cognizant of our need for this distance. As she puts it, people are brought together who do not know each other intimately "and in most cases do not care to know each other in that fashion." But this distance does not suggest indifference or disregard; it protects privacy, which is harder to come by in a city than in a small town or rural area where, instead, public life might be more in need of protection. In fact, Jacobs insists that togetherness as a city planning ideal is destructive to urban life since it operates as an artificial demand that people come together, without regard for the spontaneity and diversity of public life. Her example is a model village in Pittsburgh, where the houses are arranged in colonies around a common space with lawns, playgrounds, and a residents' club. The insularity of the complex and its middle-class homogeneity lead Jacobs to conclude: "There is no public life here, in any city sense. There are differing degrees of extended private life."[1]

The loose associations of a neighborhood are necessary in themselves and not as acquaintanceships that will one day turn into friendships. Jacobs insists they can endure for decades in their casual form and this is something to applaud. The distance in public relationships allows us to resist the inevitable homogenization and conformism of social groups and safeguard privacy. At the same time, sidewalk life generates an essential, if limited, sense of obligation and commitment to others in the neighborhood. A public identity develops through this commitment that builds the trust required for a neighborhood to become a resource in times of need. Neighbors cultivate an "assumption of support" through repeated encounters with others on the sidewalk.[2]

Jacobs gives her own examples of trust-building from the 1950s when she lived in New York City. They may seem quaint to us now for their testament to a level of trust we would find extremely rare in our contemporary urban neighborhoods. In one example, Jacobs describes the practice of leaving apartment keys with neighborhood store merchants or bar owners for friends to pick up who need access while the occupants of the apartment are not home. In another, she tells the story of a candy store owner, who, in the course of a day, supervises children crossing the street on their way to school "because he sees the need," lends umbrellas, holds packages for out-of-town neighbors, sets aside newspapers for regulars, and listens to their complaints of domestic troubles.[3]

The candy store owner is an example of what Jacobs calls "self-appointed" or "anchored" "public characters," who are instrumental in establishing trust and a sense of collective responsibility in the neighborhood. These are the shopkeepers, bartenders, and others who are present on any city block and in frequent contact with a wide circle of people in the neighborhood who regularly appear on the streets and in the stores—the network of "roving public characters." Jacobs herself became a self-appointed public character in her neighborhood of Greenwich Village when she campaigned to save a park and, years later, in Toronto, where she continued her celebrated advocacy for the vibrant life of cities.[4]

The strangers who pass through or visit from other areas of the city are as important as the leaders and regulars of a neighborhood. The goal of the urban neighborhood is not to achieve cohesiveness or self-sufficiency, like a small town which constitutes its own neighborhood, organized around a central commercial center where people gather. In a city, everyone is free to partake of multiple centers and activities—in fact, this is what cities are for, Jacobs argues; the whole point of city life is to take advantage of the wealth of choices and opportunities that a small, self-contained town cannot provide.[5] This demands the flow of change, of people coming to live in a neighborhood or departing from it. Too much change, and the neighborhood becomes unstable; too little, and it becomes stagnant.

My enthusiasm for Jacobs's discussion of neighborhoods has to do with her obvious antipathy toward self-containment. Her rich descriptions of how the fabric of a neighborhood is woven seem applicable to a range of social forms, including a community, family, or group of friends, or even a state. Jacobs recognizes the dangers of insularity and the benefits of openness in any collective form. I find especially striking the delicate balance she illuminates between stability and flow in the neighborhood. We need the store and pub owners to become neighborhood fixtures as much as we need the strangers, visitors, and new residents to prevent stasis. Surely, this is true of a nation as well.

Though I have had experiences of the kind of sidewalk life Jacobs describes, they have been intermittent. I know of neighborhoods where people care for one another within the limits set naturally by respect for neighbors' privacy and for the benefit of loose public associations, but I have rarely experienced this care myself. No doubt this is in large part due to having moved often between and within cities. An environment conducive to neighborly care—the "assumption of support" Jacobs refers to—takes time to cultivate. But I also think we are slowly forgetting the richness of a public social life, the kind Jacobs highlights so evocatively.

I think about what has brought me into contact with my neighbors over the years—front porches, gardens, snow-covered sidewalks, quiet streets—spaces that bring us into proximity over common activities like weeding, shovelling, or supervising children. The ubiquitous Toronto corner store, café, and fruit and vegetable market are also necessary to foster a sense of neighborhood, as the more we visit our local establishments, the more we identify ourselves as one of the roving public characters. But rents rise and privately owned stores and cafés close down, making way for Tim Hortons and Shoppers Drug Mart. Job insecurity and a ruthless housing market increase the transience of residents. Virtual options bring children indoors as flexible work hours bring adult jobs home.

These factors already indicate we are in danger of losing this tier of relationships that lies between our most intimate attachments and our most distant connections. It remains to be seen whether a long-term pandemic will increase or lessen the risk. For the time being we have little choice but to work from home and avoid crowded public spaces. But this may mean the neighborhood gets another chance.

Perhaps our most important task is to remember what we need, to avoid what Jacobs calls the "mass amnesia" that accompanies any dark age.[6]

AT THE CAFÉ

Sidewalk life is one manifestation of our social impulse, drawing us out of privacy to join in what Edith Stein calls the "experiential current" of human togetherness.[1] Café life is another. Here, too, we find a profusion of minute details whose sum is no small thing—a place in the world.

I began my café habit as a graduate student in the days before mocha lattes and Wi-Fi, and have continued the practice for some twenty-five years as a regular at more than a dozen cafés in several different cities. I usually have two or three favorites wherever I am; the one I choose depends on my mood or the circumstances of the day. I bring essays to grade, a book to read, a manuscript to work on, or administrative tasks. When I travel, I do the same—seek out the café with the best "culture" (according to my taste) and become a temporary regular.

The first pleasure of café life is its sensuous elements. The sounds of clattering cups and saucers merge with background music and the rise and fall of voices. The idiosyncratic expressions of faces and gestures of bodies in the room are always interesting distractions when I need them, as are the conversations I overhear unwillingly. The air is permeated with the aroma of coffee and croissants. These are the delightful accents of a public realm we join when we occupy a seat in a café. The second pleasure, in my view, is the opportunity to escape the isolation of solitary work. Judging from the growth of "coworking" spaces—essentially cafés intended for people working alone on laptops or together on group projects—I am not the only one who values this opportunity.

Every café is a unique public space with its own culture and atmosphere. Like a very small country, it is shaped not only by history, governing bodies, and ordinary citizens but also by design and vision. These factors determine whether a café's culture is friendly or reserved, artsy or businesslike, and casual or formal, welcoming or intimidating. How a café contributes to the fabric of public life is a study in itself. We have to take into account a myriad of details related to the physical space and its occupants on any given day: the configuration of tables and chairs, the demeanor of the servers, and the social habits and individual personalities of the customers. All of these details affect the public life of a café.

I am fascinated by how we move from being an individual when we enter a café to becoming an integrated part of the social body (or not, as is sometimes the case) during the course of our stay. The shift naturally occurs with the first flicker of communication between patrons—eye contact and the nod or smile that indicates we acknowledge one another's presence. Under the right conditions—proximity, interest, mood—we typically move on to brief comments that indicate some point of commonality. In Toronto (and maybe everywhere) the weather is our best proof that we inhabit the same world. Whether we are coping with a heat wave or a snow storm, we chat about the weather with strangers because it guarantees a common experience, even if our feelings about it differ.

If the association ends there, we have at the very least recognized we are both in the world, and this is not nothing. To comment on the weather every day with strangers for a lifetime would not be an insignificant ritual of species-recognition. But most of us move on. We find something besides the weather to reveal what is common to us. Children (and pets) have a magnetic effect, drawing us into conversations we would not have otherwise. When children enter a café with a parent or caregiver they become an instant focal point. They are without the reserve that urbanites have learned—the "blasé" attitude that Georg Simmel says protects us from too much stimulation in a metropolis[2]—so they smile indiscriminately and share their joys and sorrows with anyone who pays attention to them. As we are drawn irresistibly into their circle, we acknowledge anyone else who has been invited into this temporary social configuration. When a child becomes a café regular, the adults start to feel some responsibility for her, as Jane Jacobs's candy store owner did for the children he supervised crossing the street; there was a need for it and he was there. We stop the child from getting her fingers caught in the doorway or from falling off a bench when the parent turns away for a second. Here we have a perfect instance of social care generated by common feeling and the fact of our presence together in a public place.

If it is not a child that brings us together, we find something else. At a long, shared table, more common now in busy cafés that want to encourage conversation and discourage laptop use, the progression from the weather to a more substantive conversation is made easier by proximity; we find it more difficult to ignore someone sharing our table. The book I open, the sketchpad my tablemate retrieves from his bag, or the front headlines of a newspaper being read across the table can spark a conversation. The next time we happen to be there together, we have a basis for further discussion. In this way, visit by visit, conversation by conversation, we expand our repertoire of what we have in common, whether opinions, interests, complaints, perspectives, feelings, or experiences. Before long we may be disclosing snapshots of our life histories.

Or not. As Jacobs notes, public relationships, as opposed to more intimate attachments, are casual or loose associations that tend to defend the border between public and private. My interactions with other regulars at the cafés I frequent have not led to friendships, and I have not expected them to. I don't get together with them outside the space of the café. I don't always know their names or chat with them about anything beyond the weather or the morning's subway delay. What we have in common is the café—a public space familiar enough that we feel we belong there but a space that has its limits.

I have not yet mentioned the café owners, managers, and servers, who play the most critical role in establishing whether a café's culture is hospitable or indifferent. They are the "anchored" public characters Jacobs writes about with such affection in her analysis of the neighborhood. In my history of café life, two establishments stand out for their exemplary role in building a neighborhood community, both owned by remarkable people committed to welcoming patrons with small acts of care and generosity. In response, the regulars at these cafés felt some responsibility for the spaces themselves and protected their respective cultures.

I spent considerable time at one of these cafés when I lived two blocks away from it. I knew all the baristas by name and chatted with the owner and her daughters from time to time. We asked enough of each other to know about significant family crises or work-related dilemmas.

When the owner sold the business, I went to the closing party and lamented the end of an era with all the other regulars, because this is how it feels when we belong to a public space and set down roots, only to have to uproot and search for another place to belong.

The other café also became a public home to me for a number of years, until it, too, closed. I could never enter it without thinking of the *Cheers* theme song—everyone who worked there did know my name. The owner was like the quintessential bartender who listens sympathetically to the chatter of his customers, but also like an Italian grandmother—urging us to eat, giving advice, and pouring more coffee. He would sit with me from time to time and listen to me complain of student plagiarism or tell me about staffing woes. We would peer across each other's foreign worlds in the space of this new one unfolding between the walls of a café.

In both of these cases, what mattered was not the level of closeness in the relationships with owners, servers, or other regulars. Our lives touched on a relatively small point—the fact of a place in which we gathered together and to which we all belonged to one degree or another. What mattered was that I could leave my home and be greeted by name in a public place. I think this is a poignant illustration of what Barthes means when he says distance must be understood as respect, "irrigated by tender feeling."

AT THE MARKET

On Saturday mornings I like to meet a friend at the St. Lawrence Market in downtown Toronto. We have an early breakfast at Paddington's diner before we make our way through the crowded aisles between produce vendors, towing our canvas shopping carts. My friend is a market veteran; he knows his favorite vendors by name, and their cheerful greetings are followed by quick discussions about which vegetables are in season and how best to prepare them. As I follow him from one stand to the next, he introduces me to the culture of this unique space, and I happily assimilate.

Trust and conviviality are evident among the daily habits of the market. The greetings that hail my friend are extended to me. At one stall, a vendor who has worked at the market since he was fourteen is introduced to me by my friend in a lively Italian exchange that ends with the best selections of his wares for me, accompanied by a string of well wishes for the day. At another table, laden with gourds of all colors and shapes, a vendor spends five minutes explaining how to pick the best butternut squash. Look at the shape, he instructs me patiently, if the bottom is too bulbous, it will be full of seeds. And check the stem—if it is slightly soft around the edges, the squash is too ripe. He does not sell me a product, rather, he exhibits pride in his expertise growing it. There is dignity in this and we establish a rapport around it.

Every time I go to the market, I am overcome by the pleasure of the experience. It isn't only my sensuous enjoyment of the colors and textures of the fruit and vegetables, and my appreciation of the friendliness of the vendors; it is the fact that these sentiments are shared. If Arendt is right, we share a "common sense" that unites all our other senses, and this prevents us from having an idiosyncratic, therefore unreliable, sense experience. Sensuosity is infectious. Everyone at the market is caught up in a convivial attitude; it permeates the air—*this is how we are when we are here together*. We talk to strangers because a tradition of generosity and hospitality invites us to do so. We drop our urban street reserve, relax our poker faces. We would have to try very hard to resist the seduction of the market conviviality.

We are gradually being forced to use automatic checkouts in our grocery stores as human cashiers are eliminated one by one. To many this may seem an insignificant loss of human interaction; in a large urban center, most of us frequent a number of different stores and don't establish relationships with any one cashier. But this is not the case for everyone. There are cashiers who look out for their regulars, who carry on disjointed conversations over days or weeks, and who may be the only people a regular speaks to in a day. They must exert an effort to counteract the inhospitable atmosphere of the chain store and to reverse the effects of the indifferent faces of their customers.

I leave the market thinking about Franco Berardi's phrase "the eros in everyday life." He uses "eros" in the broadest sense, alluding to the pleasure of relating to others, a relational enjoyment that he thinks we are in danger of losing since workplace productivity has absorbed all our desires.[1] We have to fight to maintain the infectious conviviality that a common sense gives rise to. We can't just wait for it to happen.

CARE

I have never heard anyone express how meaningful the experience of caring for a body can be. When I helped care for my dying father a number of years ago, I didn't expect to want to care for him or to feel that caring for him was a gift to me. He didn't need medical care, since he had no official diagnosis and did not show serious signs of illness other than difficulty breathing, which was alleviated with an oxygen supply; he simply became less and less interested in eating.

I felt a profound sense of tenderness toward my father's increasingly frail body. The act of caring for him pulled me out of the world and into the diminishing circle of his existence, where the comfort of words and affection flowed instinctively and unselfconsciously. On the last evening of his life, the three women who knew him best—his wife and daughters—gathered around him as he lay on his bed. He was restless with the effort of breathing and perhaps sensed the approach of death. We massaged his back, stroked his hands and forehead, and soothed him with endearments. All of us mothers, our hands were more than familiar with the language of comfort; the memories of those other times—when we wiped a fevered forehead or embraced the child who fell off his bicycle—were impressed on our bodies.

The love manifest in care for a body may be the most selfless and at the same time the most meaningful for the giver, yet many of us never get to experience this unexpected gift. I don't mean to romanticize care and minimize what I imagine are the most difficult aspects of care work: to witness the pain and indignities of illness and death, cope with the fear or belligerence of patients, and handle the worst of what bodies and minds do when they break down. I don't know if my narrative would change if I had to empty bedpans or restrain an aggressive patient with dementia, but I persist in thinking there is a dimension of care that is pure gift—to the giver and to the recipient.

Care requires touch, tenderness, compassion—these are sensitive accompaniments to our relations with others. Love is implicated, but care also exceeds love's bounds, since love is something we feel and care is something we do. Though we can also define care as a feeling of concern for someone or something, I am more interested in care as the work we do to look after one another. Love is not necessarily required for this work unless we think of love in its broadest sense—a benevolent, compassionate orientation toward others. We could love someone without being able to care for her, and we could care for someone without loving her. But I suspect that once we take care of a body, it is difficult not to experience love for her, and conversely, without at least a little love, it is difficult to take care of a body. We may want to provide care for someone because we love her, but we may also love someone because we provide care for her. Consider the example of infant care: we take for granted that a biological bond with infants is the foundation of our love for them, but surely the continual care of small bodies, entirely dependent on us, is enough to foster attachment, regardless of our relation to them. We come to know every detail of an infant's body, become attuned to every little alteration, every sign of distress or delight, and this intimate knowledge elicits our care *and* our love. This speaks to the unique joy of being needed by someone.

That we all need care is obvious given the fragility of human existence and our absolute dependence on one another for physical and mental survival. The question of who will provide it is less obvious. Historically, care has been women's work, paid or unpaid, public or private. We have nursed our children, the sick and dying, our ailing parents, and managed our homes, as well as the organizations or institutions responsible for care. Everything has changed now that women are allowed to do other things besides care work, and men have only picked up a bit of the slack. The care deficit that followed women's mass movement into the workforce during the latter half of the twentieth century has worsened with the effects of intensified market capitalism and accelerated technology. Heightened work stress, the necessity of dual incomes in families, weakened community ties, and the virtualization of the social, all mean that we need more care while there are fewer to offer it. Care work is not something we do well for instrumental reasons. It is incompatible with the drive for profit. Obviously, care is also hard to provide without the actual presence of a body—young, old, sickly, frail, injured, bloody, smelly, hungry, dying. When we are not directly confronted by the need for care, we are not likely to respond to it.

There is a context to care—it has conditions either conducive or hostile to its work. Bodies demand our time; they don't succumb to illness when it is convenient for our work schedules. Babies can arrive at the worst of times and so can death. The aging process does not pause for us when we are absorbed by a project, in need of energy and good health, and freedom from distractions. The body is demanding and impatient, inconsiderate of our need for sleep or concentration. The one who cares needs replenishment.

But we don't have time anymore so we pay others to do the caring. This would not be a bad arrangement if we organized it around principles of fairness and dignity. If women once did most of the unpaid care work in the private sphere, they now do most of the underpaid care work in the public sphere in addition to much of the unpaid care work at home. Nothing highlights this more starkly than the current pandemic, since the lockdowns require the suspension of all jobs other than "essential services." Suddenly we discover that the jobs most vital for the basic functioning of society are largely held by women, and the majority of these are women of color. Furthermore, these essential jobs are also among the lowest paid. According to one report, nine out of ten nurses and nursing assistants and more than two-thirds of grocery store checkout and fast-food counter employees in the United States are women. Of 5.8 million health care workers earning less than 30,000 per year, 83 percent are women and half of these are nonwhite women.[1]

As I write, the residents of long-term care homes in my province are dying at unusually high rates not only because they are the most vulnerable to Covid-19 but because of the appalling conditions that render some of these homes incapable of handling an outbreak. The Canadian Armed Forces, called in to assist with outbreaks in five long-term care homes, has released a report that exposes an egregious disregard for basic health care principles and practices. The report details chronic staff shortages, the use of contaminated catheters, aggressive feeding practices that cause choking, rotten food, and roach infestations.[2] It is perhaps not surprising that deaths by Covid-19 are four times more likely in for-profit than in nonprofit or city-run homes.[3]

It is a gross understatement to say these conditions are hostile to care. There are less horrific manifestations of what happens when conditions for care are poor, but their cumulative effects are also worrying. Our society is overwhelmed by a multitude of unmet physical and mental needs, with varying degrees of severity, a predicament that exposes the contradiction between the happiness our relatively wealthy, liberal democracies promise and the reality of our day-to-day lives. We can't always find someone to help us move a heavy piece of furniture, change a flat tire, take care of our cats, or water our plants when we go on vacation. If we live alone, we worry about getting ill and not having anyone to help us. The insufficiency of mental health care was already in evidence before the pandemic exacerbated psychological struggles through isolation and loneliness. Our cities have growing populations of homeless people living on the streets only because they are mentally ill and have nowhere to go. Our universities keep increasing funding for student mental health resources. I think this is where the loss of community or neighborhood relationships is felt most keenly—the "assumption of support" to which Jane Jacobs alluded can no longer be assumed.

The trouble is, we all need to be cared for in one way or another, but no one is entitled to expect others to meet their needs. Care is a gift—we have to rely on someone's desire to give it. In Simone Weil's enumeration of "the needs of the soul," she argues it makes no sense to say we have rights and obligations at the same time, for whether we have one or the other depends on our point of view. I have an obligation to you, and from this vantage point, you are the one with rights. Conversely, you have an obligation to me and from your vantage point I am the one with rights. Weil's point, however, is that I only need to think of my obligations to you—that is my vantage point. If all of us take seriously our own obligations, we will not need to demand our rights.[4]

Unfortunately, we don't live in a world where everyone takes their obligation to care for others seriously enough to experience the reciprocity of their gift.

FRIENDSHIP

There is a striking passage about friendship in Simone Weil's brilliant analysis of oppression, written in 1934 during the rising nationalist and authoritarian fervor of Hitler's new leadership in Germany. Given the historical context, we might be surprised by her declaration: "We should possess, over and above liberty, a still more precious good; for if nothing is more odious than the humiliation and degradation of man by man, nothing is so beautiful or so sweet as friendship." Weil has just explained that even if servitude is the natural condition of humankind—for we are enslaved by progress—nothing can stop us from feeling "born for liberty." This is not the freedom that gives us what we want without having to overcome obstacles; freedom for Weil is the ability to act in accordance with the movements of our minds—our thoughts and judgments. Such autonomy is an ideal we will never achieve in reality, but we must aim for it anyway, Weil says, "in the hope of attaining a less imperfect liberty than is our present condition."[1]

It is no small thing to be denied autonomy by a source outside our own minds. This is the lesson of all forms of fascism we seem resistant to learning. Thus, we might be skeptical of the idea that friendship is "a still more precious good" than freedom. It follows that we would be better off enslaved with friends than to be free and friendless, better to have companionship without autonomy than to be lonely with all the freedom we need to act on our wills. Yet slavery has always been upheld as among the worst conditions for a human being. To put friendship above freedom feels like a travesty.

Friendship has been eclipsed by the "intimate partner" relationship. We define intimate love as a romantic, sexual relationship and have built a vast vocabulary around the practice of coupledom, honoring its various stages and milestones. But when it comes to friendship, our vocabulary thins out. We ask our acquaintances and potential lovers: Are you seeing anyone now? Are you in a relationship? Do you have a partner?—but we are not inquiring about a friendship or expressing curiosity about what friends might be to one another. When someone asks about a new attachment we are forming, we might say, *We're just friends*, as though friendship is merely a consolation prize. Do we know what a friend is? Do we know what a friend can be?

I don't think we can answer these questions in the abstract. When I think of my own closest friends, what springs to mind first is the unmitigated pleasure of seeing their faces, hearing their voices, and expressing our mutual affection. I marvel at how beautiful my friends are, a beauty far beyond the dictates of cultural standards of physical attractiveness that elicits whatever is beautiful in me. This is what love does for us, as Diotima explains in her famous speech to Socrates in Plato's *Symposium*. Love "gives birth in beauty" or perhaps—given the ambiguity of the original Greek preposition in this phrase—love gives birth "in the presence of beauty."[2] When we encounter someone beautiful, we give birth to what we have been "carrying" inside us:[3] the thoughts we didn't know we had until they surfaced in conversation or the hidden facets of our characters illuminated only in the presence of a friend.

There is a material, sensuous context to my interactions with friends—a worldliness. Now that a pandemic has reduced our interactions to phone conversations, we understand better the need for this worldly context—the colors, sounds, and textures that flesh out our interactions and affirm what we share with our senses. I normally meet my friends in cafés. One friend meets me every week at the same café, preferably at the same table overlooking a busy Toronto street, our surroundings not merely a backdrop but also a catalyst for thinking together. Our observations of sidewalk life or the idiosyncrasies of those chatting around us work their way into our conversations. Another friend meets me in a library where we work silently together for hours, occasionally looking up from our books to share a moving or perplexing passage—the entire day an expression of gratitude for our philosophical friendship.

A remarkable feature of these visits with my friends is the synthesis of our moods over the course of our time together. We may arrive tired, in despair over the state of the world, but we leave enlivened by one another's company and by the conversation that flows between us; emotional and sensuous states are infectious. We know that whatever we must face, we will face together. This is trust.

To be in a friend's home is an experience of its own—a gesture of trust. The rarity of the event might be unique to contemporary urban life—the din and speed of the city means our homes are more private than they would need to be in a less congested environment. Add to this the relentless pressure of work and the stress of getting around the city, and we may find the café visit on the way home more convenient than making a messy apartment presentable. But there is no substitute for being among friends in their most private spaces, where the *who* I love is magnified in the objects of daily use—favourite coffee mugs and newspapers, art and mementos—and in the evidence of habitual movements, from a creaky floorboard to a worn chair. Hospitality is a gift of profound generosity.

This is also what it means to touch someone "on the inside part," to recall Beloved's words to Paul D.[4] Friendship has an eros of its own; desire and enjoyment draw us into the life of a friend and hold us there. Whether this eros involves the intermingling of genitalia seems to matter less when friend-love rather than couple-love is our standard of measure. I struggle for the right words here, since I don't think we have a name for what I want to call intimate love for the dearest of friends, though these relationships are not sexual. Given the range of closeness the term "friend" implies, we ought to expand our vocabulary and the imagination to go with it. If the value of any form of love is its depth, intensity, and generosity, we should be able to dispense with the hierarchy between couple-love and friend-love. Only then will we understand what a friend can be.

LOVE

Our greatest social need is love. If there were no such thing as love, we wouldn't even have a word for loneliness, since love and intimacy go hand in hand. This is not to say we can't be lonely when we are loved. Loneliness is a craving for intimacy—and by this, I mean something more than the sexual kind—but intimacy varies in form and intensity. When we are without one form, another may compensate, as when the brain boosts the functioning sense organs of a blind person to make up for the loss of sight. When we are young and without close friends, the love of a parent or another adult may partially compensate. When we are old we may lose those who love us best, yet experience a caregiver's kindness or the unconditional devotion of a pet, and this might be enough to take the edge off loneliness. It follows that we find the most severe loneliness among those who are without love altogether, in any of its forms or manifestations, including acts of care, kindness, and tenderness.

When I say we need love, I mean we need our existence affirmed by another. To be loved means someone knows and values *who* we are—the sum of the thoughts, feelings, choices, and actions that constitutes our characters over time. As Michel de Montaigne famously said about his beloved friend Étienne de la Boétie: "If I were pressed to say why I love him, I feel that my only reply could be: 'Because it was he, because it was I.'"[1] There is no reason or purpose for this love; we are brought by chance into proximity with another life and we become attached. Something in you speaks to something in me—we are moved by the same things, share certain interests and an orientation toward the world. Love means we become an integral part of each other's life stories.

What we do with these feelings of love for others—how love is expressed in our behavior toward them—is another matter. This is where all the vicissitudes of our characters and psychological histories come into play, since love is always limited by who we are and by what we can do. We can't demand that our loved ones fulfill all our needs for care or companionship because they have limits, just as we have limits in our ability to meet their needs. Neither can we expect our intimate friends to know us in an absolute sense, to see all the hidden sides of us, for we can't even know ourselves in such fullness. This is why we need a wider social world, beyond what is offered to us by those we love the most. How unreliable my sense of self would be, how one-dimensional and static, if I interacted with only one or two loved ones, and thus experienced myself through their limited vision of me. I need a plurality of others to know me as more than this or that one thing and who will alter my character, smooth its edges, bit by bit, simply by being not-me. I also need them to provide a level of care and tenderness none of us can do without.

But first we need love, and there is no substitute for this need, though giving love may appease it. The affirmation of who we are, our worth as lovable persons, and our emotional attachments to others come before any material manifestations of intimacy. If I have to choose between the friend who will care for me when I am ill and the love of a friend who understands me in the undefinable depths of who I am, I will choose the latter. The distinction is important at a time when the social infrastructure necessary for care work is fracturing. In a perfect world we might be granted both love and care.

We have an impulse to love and to seek the intimacy love suggests. Our desire for attachment can be powerful even if the intensity of this impulse varies from person to person. We crave an experience of fusion, with bodies, minds, and even the natural world—to be so deeply a part of someone or something that we don't know where one of us ends and the other begins.

I return again to Morrison's ghost-girl, Beloved, who longs to be loved unconditionally by the mother she lost: "I am looking for the join . . . I want to join . . . I am alone . . . I want to be the two of us . . . I want the join."[2]

THE JOIN

I know the exhilaration of "the join."

When I performed in a choir, feeling one with the sound, my own voice merging with every other voice to produce perfect, four-part harmony. We were a unit; no discordant tone, no individual voice stood out from another. One shrill soprano or self-promoting tenor would have broken the seamless fusion. Choristers must obey the laws of harmony and tempo, for the music is everything and the individual singer is nothing apart from the whole. We lost our separate selves in that euphoric moment when the sound spiralled to the ceiling, when we became the music as the dancer's body becomes movement or the painter's hand becomes the landscape.

When I have loved, feeling my body open to another in a moment of pure vulnerability. I know this extraordinary pleasure—when love and passion are an expanding territory, when boundaries dissolve and we momentarily forget that we exist separately. The forgetting is not even conscious, since consciousness seems suspended; it is a bodily oblivion. We merge, then return to our separate selves. Love joins us, then gives us back to ourselves, more cherished than we believed we could be.

When I have "a friend of my mind." This is how Sixo, a character in *Beloved*, describes the woman he loves, the friend who gathers all the "pieces" of him together and returns them in the right order.[1] I borrow this phrase to describe the intimate rapport between friends who generate thoughts and sentiments larger than the sum of their parts, and arrive at mutual understanding. Like choristers, and lovers, the moment of our exhilaration this time is a fusion not of voices or bodies but of insight and emotion.

These brief experiences of what can feel like pure unity may well be events through which we memorialize our original fusion to another's body. This would explain the melancholic aftermath of the join—each one another step in the work of mourning that initial loss.

The join is always fleeting; if we forget this, we risk not being able to return to ourselves.

WITNESS

Sheila Heti's eccentric short story "My Life Is a Joke" is narrated by a character who comes back to life in order to say something she left unsaid. She tells the reader that she died alone without a witness; she never married and had no children. When her high-school boyfriend asked her to marry him because he thought everyone needed a witness in life, she rejected him: "I didn't like his idea of what a wife was for—someone to just hang around and watch your life unfold." He gets his witness anyway—many, in fact—when he marries a woman with a large family, has a child, and settles into a community surrounded by extended family and friends. They will watch his life unfold, see his failures, and love him anyway. Heti's narrator comes back from the dead to tell us that she now understands: "It is no small thing to have someone who loves you see your life, and discuss it with you every night."[1]

The story ends with a simple insight: "How beautiful to be seen."[2] I take this to be Heti's point: we need a witness for both the dramatic and the mundane events of our daily lives, someone to whom we can relate the contents of the day, however trivial, and our thoughts and feelings about them. This is what I have missed when living alone, along with the sounds of life in another room.

I want to interpret Heti's insight broadly. Having a witness does not necessarily mean living with someone we can greet when we go home at the end of the day—I don't want to believe her narrator is merely advising us to marry or cohabit—it means *living with* others in the most profound sense of the "with," watching a life unfold over time. This is not a passive witnessing but an attentive one; we must be fully present to one another.

How beautiful it is to be seen.

NOTES

Preface

1. Arundhati Roy, "The Pandemic Is a Portal," *Financial Times*, April 3, 2020, https://www.ft.com/content/10d8f5e8-74eb-11ea-95fe-fcd274e920ca.

The Paradox (I)

1. Maev Kennedy, "Loo with a View," *Guardian*, December 4, 2003, https://www.theguardian.com/uk/2003/dec/04/arts.artsnews.
2. "Six Things You Need to Know about Monica Bonvicini," *Phaidon*, https://ca.phaidon.com/agenda/art/articles/2014/june/17/six-things-you-need-to-know-about-monica-bonvicini/.

The Lonely I

1. See Thomas Dumm, *Loneliness as a Way of Life* (Cambridge: Harvard University Press, 2010); Olivia Laing, *The Lonely City* (London: Picador, 2016); Emily White, *Lonely: Learning to Live with Solitude* (Toronto: McClelland & Stewart, 2010).
2. Clark E. Moustakas, *Loneliness* (Pickle Partners Publishing, 2016), Kindle, Location 171.
3. Ibid., Location 82.
4. Marissa Korda, "The Loneliness Project," http://thelonelinessproject.org/.
5. Diane Enns, "The Other L Word," *Philosophers Zone*, interview by Joe Gelonesi, ABC, April 23, 2017, audio, https://www.abc.net.au/

radionational/programs/philosopherszone/the-other-l-word-loneliness/8454692.

Stigma

1 Sigmund Freud, "The 'Uncanny'," (1919) in *The Standard Edition of the Complete Psychological Works of Sigmund Freud Volume XVII (1917–1919): An Infantile Neurosis and Other Works*, ed. and trans. James Strachey (London: Vintage, 2001), 217–56.

2 Ibid., 233.

3 "Vulnerable," *Online Etymology Dictionary*, https://www.etymonline.com/word/vulnerable.

4 Rollo May, *Man's Search for Himself* (New York: W.W. Norton and Co., 1953), 15.

In the Village

1 Susan Pinker, *The Village Effect: How Face-to-Face Contact Can Make Us Healthier, Happier, and Smarter* (Vintage Canada, 2015), 29.

In the Loneliness Laboratory

1 George Monbiot, "The Age of Loneliness Is Killing Us," *The Guardian*, October 14, 2014, https://www.theguardian.com/commentisfree/2014/oct/14/age-of-loneliness-killing-us.

2 See John Bowlby, *Attachment. Attachment and Loss*, Vol. 1 (New York: Basic Books, 1969); Clark E. Moustakas, *Loneliness* (Pickle Partners Publishing, 2016), Kindle; Robert S. Weiss, *Loneliness: The Experience of Emotional and Social Isolation* (Cambridge: MIT Press, 1975); and Gregory Zilboorg, "Loneliness," *The Atlantic Monthly* (January, 1938): 45–54.

3 See Joseph Hartog, Ralph Audy, and Yedudi A. Cohen, *The Anatomy of Loneliness* (New York: International Universities Press, 1980); Letitia Anne Peplau and Daniel Perlman, *Loneliness: A Sourcebook of Current Theory, Research and Therapy* (New York: John Wiley & Sons, 1982); and Leroy S. Rouner, ed., *Loneliness* (Notre Dame: University of Notre Dame Press, 1998).

4 Peplau and Perlman, *Loneliness: A Sourcebook*, 2.

5 Ibid., 9–11.

6 Ibid., 3–5.

7 Ibid., 4.

8 Olivia Sagan and Eric Miller, eds., *Narratives of Loneliness: Multidisciplinary Perspectives from the 21st Century* (New York: Routledge, 2017), 2.

9 Epictetus, "Enchiridion," in *Epictetus: Discourses and Selected Writings*, trans. Robert Dobbin (London: Penguin Books, 2008), 234.

10 Judith Shulevitz, "The Lethality of Loneliness," *The New Republic*, May 13, 2013, https://newrepublic.com/article113176/science-loneliness-how-isolation-can-kill-you.

11 John T. Cacioppo and William Patrick, *Loneliness: Human Nature and the Need for Social Connection* (New York: W.W. Norton & Company, 2008), 12, 106.

12 Shulevitz, "The Lethality of Loneliness."

13 Pinker, *The Village Effect*, 206.

14 Ibid., 202.

15 Cacioppo and Patrick, *Loneliness*, 16.

16 Ibid., 15–16.

17 Ibid., 34, 37.

18 Ibid., 31, 34, 37.

19 Lars Svendsen, *A Philosophy of Loneliness* (London: Reaktion Books, 2017), 135.

20 Ibid., 58–9, 129.

21 Pinker, *The Village Effect*, 270–1.

22 Cacioppo and Patrick, *Loneliness*, 19.

23 Ibid., 229.

The Paradox (II)

1 Toni Morrison, *Beloved* (New York: Plume, 1987), 116.

What Is Loneliness?

1. I am referring here to Irving Singer's concept of "bestowal" in his study of love. See "Appraisal and Bestowal," in *The Nature of Love*, Vol. I: Plato to Luther, 2nd ed. (Chicago: University of Chicago Press, 1984).

2. Frieda Fromm-Reichmann, "Loneliness," *Psychiatry* 22, no. 1 (1959): 1. This patient fully recovered and later wrote a fictionalized account of her treatment by Fromm-Reichmann. See Hannah Green, *I Never Promised You a Rose Garden: A Novel* (New York: St. Martin's Press, 1964).

3. Fromm-Reichmann, "Loneliness," 3.

4. Ibid., 3.

5. Ibid., 3.

6. Harry Stack Sullivan, *The Interpersonal Theory of Psychiatry* (New York: Norton, 1953), 290. Quoted in Fromm-Reichmann, "Loneliness," 3.

7. Fromm-Reichmann, "Loneliness," 1, 6.

8. Ibid., 2–3.

9. Ibid., 5.

10. Ibid., 7, 5–6.

11. Ibid., 3, 5.

12. Ibid., 5.

13. Ibid., 13.

14. Hannah Arendt, *The Human Condition* (Chicago: The University of Chicago Press, 1958), 198–9; 182–4.

15. Hannah Arendt, *The Origins of Totalitarianism*, New Edition (New York: Harcourt Brace & Company, 1973), 478.

16. Ibid., 474–5.

The Alienation of Gregor Samsa

1. Franz Kafka, *Metamorphosis and Other Stories*, trans. Michael Hofmann (London: Penguin Books, 2007), 87–8.

2. Ibid., 136.

The Philosopher Stands Alone

1. Tennessee Williams, *Orpheus Descending*, 1958, 26, http://www.newmoontheatre.org/uploads/2/1/7/6/21764846/orpheus_edit_12-3.pdf.
2. Octavio Paz, *The Labyrinth of Solitude*, trans. Lysander Kemp, Yara Milos, Rachel Phillips Belash (New York: Grove Press, 1985), 9.
3. Ibid., 208.
4. Virginia Woolf, "On Being Ill," in *Selected Essays*, ed. David Bradshaw (Oxford: Oxford University Press, 2008), 101–10, 104.
5. Ibid., 104.
6. Moustakas, *Loneliness*, Location 82, 222, 747–57.
7. Paul Tillich, "Loneliness and Solitude," in *The Anatomy of Loneliness*, ed. Joseph Hartog et al. (New York: International Universities Press, 1980), 547–53, 551.
8. Ibid., 550, 548.
9. Ibid., 551–3.
10. Moustakas, *Loneliness*, Location 55.
11. Edith Stein, *Philosophy of Psychology and the Humanities*, trans. M. C. Baseheart and M. Sawicki (Washington, DC: ICS Publications, 2000), 145.
12. Antonio Calcagno, *Lived Experience from the Inside Out: Social and Political Philosophy in Edith Stein* (Pittsburgh, PA: Duquesne University Press, 2014), 40. See also Edith Stein, *On the Problem of Empathy*, trans. Waltraut Stein (Washington, DC: ICS Publications, 1989).
13. Jean-Paul Sartre, "The Humanism of Existentialism," *Essays in Existentialism* (New York: Citadel Press, 1993), 41.
14. Ibid., 47.
15. Jean-Paul Sartre, "Freedom and Responsibility," *Essays in Existentialism*, 64–5.
16. Sartre, "The Humanism of Existentialism," 51–2.
17. Sartre, *Being and Nothingness*, trans. Hazel E. Barnes (New York: Washington Square Press, 1992), 484.
18. Ibid., 481–2.
19. Jean-Paul Sartre, *No Exit*, in *No Exit and Three Other Plays*, trans. S. Gilbert (New York: Vintage International Edition, 1989), 45.
20. Albert Camus, "The Myth of Sisyphus," in *The Myth of Sisyphus and Other Essays*, trans. Justin O'Brien (New York: Vintage International, 1991), 121–3.

21 See especially Franz von Stuck, *Sisyphus*, oil on canvas, 1920 (Galerie Ritthaler, München), https://fineartamerica.com/featured/sisyphus-franz-von-stuck.html.

22 Albert Camus, *The Rebel: An Essay on Man in Revolt*, trans. Anthony Bower (New York: Vintage Books, 1991), 22.

23 Simone de Beauvoir, *The Ethics of Ambiguity*, trans. Bernard Frechtman (New York: Citadel Press, 1976), 8–9.

24 Camus, *The Myth of Sisyphus and Other Essays*, 3–16.

25 Friedrich Nietzsche, *Twilight of the Idols*, trans. Duncan Large (Oxford: Oxford University Press, 1998), 58.

26 Lou Salomé, *Nietzsche*, trans. Siegfried Mandel (Chicago: University of Illinois Press, 2001), 12.

27 Ibid., 10.

28 Melanie Klein, "On the Sense of Loneliness," in *Envy and Gratitude and Other Works 1946–1963*, vol. III, ed. Roger Money-Kyrle (New York: The Free Press, 1975), 311.

29 Ralph Waldo Emerson, "Self-Reliance," 13, 3, 4, 13, 18, 12, https://math.dartmouth.edu/~doyle/docs/self/self.pdf.

30 Ibid., 5, 14, 21.

31 Virginia Woolf, *A Room of One's Own*; *Three Guineas*, ed. Michèle Barrett (New York: Penguin Books, 1993), 89–90.

In the Hole

1 Lisa Guenther, *Solitary Confinement: Social Death and Its Afterlives* (Minneapolis: University of Minnesota Press, 2013), 69.

2 The CIA manual is KUBARK, 1963, 88, quoted in Guenther, *Solitary Confinement*, 82. Guenther points out that KUBARK quoted from Lilly but referred to the wrong page. See note 20, 82.

3 Lawrence E. Hinkle and Harold G. Wolff, "Communist Interrogation and Indoctrination of 'Enemies of the State'" (American Medical Association, 1956), 129, quoted in Guenther, *Solitary Confinement*, 68.

4 Atul Gawande, "Hellhole," *New Yorker*, March 30, 2009, https://www.newyorker.com/magazine/2009/03/30/hellhole.

5 Dana G. Smith, "Neuroscientists Make a Case against Solitary Confinement," *Scientific American*, November 9, 2018, https://www

.scientificamerican.com/article/neuroscientists-make-a-case-against-solitary-confinement/.
6 Guenther, *Solitary Confinement*, 164.
7 Jack Henry Abbott, *In the Belly of the Beast: Letters from Prison* (New York: Random House, 1981), 51.
8 Ibid., 52–3.

The Ambivalence of Solitude

1 Michael Finkel, "Into the Woods; How One Man Survived Alone in the Wilderness for 27 Years," *Guardian*, March 15, 2017, https://www.theguardian.com/news/2017/mar/15/stranger-in-the-woods-christopher-knight-hermit-maine.
2 Paul Willis, "This Reclusive Life: What I Learned about Solitude from My Time with Hermits," *Guardian*, October 6, 2017, https://www.theguardian.com/us-news/2017/oct/06/hermits-solitude-wilderness-new-mexico.
3 Michael Finkel, "The Strange and Curious Tale of the Last True Hermit," *GQ*, August 5, 2014, https://www.gq.com/story/the-last-true-hermit.
4 Finkel, "Into the Woods."
5 Willis, "This Reclusive Life."
6 John Haldane, in Thomas Morris, "The Philosophy of Solitude," *BBC Sounds: In Our Time*, June 19, 2014, https://www.bbc.co.uk/sounds/play/b046ntnz.
7 Arendt, *The Human Condition*, 15.
8 Plato, *Symposium*, trans. Alexander Nehamas and Paul Woodruff (Indianapolis: Hackett Publishing Co., 1989), 207A.
9 Morris, "The Philosophy of Solitude."
10 Mary Wellesley, "The Life of the Anchoress," *Discovering Literature: Medieval*, March 13, 2018, https://www.bl.uk/medieval-literature/articles/the-life-of-the-anchoress.
11 Michel de Montaigne, "Of Solitude," *Essays of Michel de Montaigne*, trans. Charles Cotton, ed. William Hazlitt, https://www.gutenberg.org/files/3600/3600-h/3600-h.htm.
12 Henry David Thoreau, *Walden*, ed. Stephen Fender (New York: Oxford University Press, 1977), 120, 123.
13 Kathryn Schulz, "The Moral Judgments of Henry David Thoreau," *New Yorker*, October 19, 2015.
14 Finkel, "The Strange and Curious Tale of the Last True Hermit."

15 Anthony Storr, *Solitude: A Return to the Self* (New York: The Free Press, 1988), xiv.
16 Fromm-Reichmann, "Loneliness," 7.
17 Ibid., 7.
18 Ibid., 6.
19 Sara Maitland, *How to Be Alone* (London: Macmillan, 2014), 25–9.
20 Ibid., 57.
21 Ibid., 91.
22 Sara Maitland, "'Savour Solitude—It Is Not the Same as Loneliness,'" *Guardian*, May 17, 2020, https://www.theguardian.com/society/2020/may/17/sara-maitland-savour-solitude-it-is-not-the-same-as-loneliness.
23 Anthony Stevens, "Anthony Storr," *Guardian*, March 20, 2001, https://www.theguardian.com/news/2001/mar/20/guardianobituaries.highereducation.
24 Storr, *Solitude*, xiv, xi–xiv.
25 Ibid., 29, 21.
26 Ibid., xiv.
27 Anthony Stevens, "Anthony Storr."
28 Hannah Arendt, *The Life of the Mind*, One-Volume Edition (New York: Harcourt, Inc, 1971), 175, 185.
29 Storr, *Solitude*, 46.
30 Ibid., xiii, 11, 18, 28.
31 Denise Ryan, "Novelist Says Loneliness Is a 'Very Privileged' Thing," *Vancouver Sun*, February 24, 2017, https://vancouversun.com/entertainment/books/novelist-says-lonesomeness-a-very-privileged-thing.

Solus

1 Susan Sontag, "Pilgrimage," in *Debriefing: Collected Stories*, ed. Benjamin Taylor (New York: Farrar, Straus and Giroux, 2017), 29.
2 May Sarton, *Journal of a Solitude* (New York: W.W. Norton & Co., 1973), 195–6.
3 Ibid., 113–14.
4 Ibid., 199, 195–6.
5 Ibid., 115, 107.
6 Ibid., 11.
7 Ibid., 108.

Alone Together

1. Sherry Turkle, "Connected, But Alone," *TED*, 2012, https://www.ted.com/talks/sherry_turkle_connected_but_alone?language=en.
2. Sherry Turkle, *Alone Together: Why We Expect More from Technology and Less from Each Other* (New York: Basic Books, 2011).
3. Stein, *Philosophy of Psychology and the Humanities*, 197, 144, 273, 133.
4. Martin Buber, *Between Man and Man*, trans. Ronald Gregor-Smith (New York: Routledge, 2002), 236–44, 242.
5. Moustakas, *Loneliness*, Location 52–6.

"Organized Loneliness"

1. Arendt, *The Origins of Totalitarianism*, 464.
2. Ibid., 473.
3. Ibid., 474.
4. Ibid., 474–5.
5. Ibid., 474.
6. Ibid., 475.
7. Ibid., 474–5.
8. Ibid., 476–7.
9. Ibid., 475; Arendt, *The Human Condition*, 76.
10. Arendt, *The Origins of Totalitarianism*, 478, 465–6, 475–6.
11. Ibid., 478.
12. Hannah Arendt, *The Promise of Politics*, ed. Jerome Kohn (New York: Schocken Books, 2005), 201.
13. Arendt, *The Human Condition*, 248–57.
14. Ibid., 154.
15. See Arendt's claim at the end of *The Human Condition* that "making, fabricating, and building" continue as human activities in the modern world, though these activities are "more and more restricted to the abilities of the artist," 323.
16. Franco "Bifo" Berardi, *The Soul at Work: From Alienation to Autonomy*, trans. Francesca Cadel and Giuseppina Mecchia (South Pasadena: Semiotext(e), 2009) 21–2. Berardi borrows the term "semiocapitalism" from Jean Baudrillard.

17 Luis Suarez-Villa, *Technocapitalism: A Critical Perspective on Technological Innovation and Corporatism* (Philadelphia: Temple University Press, 2009), 3, 32.
18 Shoshana Zuboff, "Big Other: Surveillance Capitalism and the Prospects of an Information Civilization," *Journal of Information Technology* 30 (2015): 75.
19 Suarez-Villa, *Technocapitalism*, 4.

The Tyranny of the Couple

1 K. D. M. Snell, "The Rise of Living Alone and Loneliness in History," *Social History* 42, no. 1 (2017): 18, 10.
2 Michèle Barrett and Mary McIntosh, *The Anti-social Family* (New York: Verso Press, 2015), 56.
3 Erich Fromm, *The Art of Loving* (New York: Harper & Row, Inc., 2006), 81.
4 See Claudia Card, "Against Marriage and Motherhood," *Hypatia* 11, no. 3 (Summer 1996).
5 Elizabeth Brake, *Minimizing Marriage: Marriage, Morality, and the Law* (Oxford: Oxford University Press, 2012), 5.
6 Ibid., 89, 92–4. Brake explains that "married men receive significantly higher pay than their unmarried male peers with similar levels of achievement; moreover, singles widely report being expected to work evenings and holidays, to take on assignments involving extensive travel, and otherwise being treated by employees as if their nonwork commitments were less important than those of married co-workers," 94.
7 See also Rebecca Traister, *All the Single Ladies* (New York: Simon and Schuster, 2016); Kate Bolick, *Spinster* (New York: Broadway Books, 2016); Eric Klinenberg, *Going Solo* (London: Penguin Books, 2013).
8 See Bella DePaulo, "Single People Aren't to Blame for the Loneliness Epidemic," *The Atlantic: Family*, August 28, 2018, https://www.theatlantic.com/family/archive/2018/08/single-people-arent-to-blame-for-the-loneliness-epidemic/568786/.
9 See Bella DePaulo, *How We Live Now: Redefining Home and Family in the 21st Century* (New York: Atria Books, 2015).
10 Bella DePaulo, "Why Are You Still Single?: Here's the Best Way to Answer," *Psychology Today*, blog posted July 27, 2019, https://www.psychologytoday.com/ca/blog/living-single/201907/why-are-you-single-here-are-some-my-favorite-answers.

NOTES

11 Lea Melandri, *Love and Violence: The Vexatious Factors of Civilization*, trans. Antonio Calcagno (Albany: SUNY Press, 2019), 37.

At Home

1 Sameer Rahim, "Doris Lessing: In Her Own Words," *The Telegraph*, Book News, November 17, 2013, https://www.telegraph.co.uk/culture/books/booknews/10455645/Doris-Lessing-in-her-own-words.html.
2 Virginia Woolf, *To the Lighthouse* (London: Grafton Books, 1977), 39.

The Antisocial Family

1 Kate Chopin, *The Awakening and Selected Stories* (New York: Penguin Books, 1984), 51.
2 Roland Barthes, *How to Live Together: Novelistic Simulations of Some Everyday Spaces*, trans. Kate Briggs (New York: Columbia University Press, 2013), 5.
3 Ibid., 5.
4 Shivani Vora, "How Neil Patrick Harris and David Burtka Spend Their Sundays," *New York Times*, June 14, 2019,

https://www.nytimes.com/2019/06/14/nyregion/neil-patrick-harris-david-burtka.html?searchResultPosition=1.
5 Barthes, *How to Live Together,* 5.
6 Storr, *Solitude*, xiii.
7 Barrett and McIntosh, *The Anti-Social Family*, 21–3.
8 Ibid., 29.
9 Ibid., 171.
10 Ibid., 79–80, 77.
11 Ibid., 133–4; 144–52.

Against Community

1 See "Bolivian Mennonites Jailed for Serial Rapes," *BBC News*, August 26, 2011, https://www.bbc.com/news/world-latin-america-14688458;

Andres Schipani, "'The Work of the Devil': Crime in a Remote Religious Community," *Guardian*, September 10, 2009, https://www.theguardian.com/world/2009/sep/10/mennonites-rape-bolivia; Jean Friedman-Rudovsky, "The Ghost Rapes of Bolivia," *Vice*, December 22, 2013, https://www.vice.com/en_ca/article/4w7gqj/the-ghost-rapes-of-bolivia-000300-v20n8.

2 Friedman-Rudovsky, "The Ghost Rapes of Bolivia."
3 Jean Friedman-Rudovsky, "The Verdict in Bolivia's Shocking Case of the Mennonite Rapes," *Time*, August 17, 2011, http://content.time.com/time/world/article/0,8599,2087711,00.html.
4 Friedman-Rudovsky, "The Ghost Rapes of Bolivia."
5 I have written more extensively on my Mennonite background in "For the Love of Paradox: Mennonite Morality and Philosophy," in *Religious Upbringing and the Costs of Freedom: Personal and Philosophical Essays*, eds. Peter Caws and Stefani Jones (Penn State University Press, 2010), and *Love in the Dark: Philosophy by Another Name* (Columbia University Press, 2016).
6 Ferdinand Tönnies, *Community and Society*, trans. Charles P. Loomis (New York: Harper, 1963), 47, 65, 49, quoted in Zygmunt Bauman, *Community: Seeking Safety in an Insecure World* (Oxford: Polity Press, 2001), 10.
7 Franco "Bifo" Berardi, *And: Phenomenology of the End* (Semiotext[e], 2015), 67–8.
8 Kwame Anthony Appiah, *The Lies That Bind: Rethinking Identity* (New York: Liveright Publishing Co., 2018), 3.
9 Bauman, *Community*, 3.
10 Arendt, *The Life of the Mind*, 88.
11 Roberto Esposito, *Terms of the Political: Community, Immunity, Biopolitics*, trans. Rhiannon Noel Welch (New York: Fordham University Press, 2013), 61, 62.
12 Bauman, *Community*, 17–18.
13 Ibid., 117.
14 Ibid., 5.
15 Amartya Sen, *Identity and Violence: The Illusion of Destiny* (New York: Penguin Books, 2006), xv–xvi.
16 Ibid., 2.

Nostalgia

1 *The Farewell*, dir. Lulu Wang, August, 2019, Ray Productions, https://www.imdb.com/title/tt8637428/.

"The Soul at Work"

1. James Bloodworth, "I Worked in an Amazon Warehouse: Bernie Sanders Is Right to Target Them," *Guardian*, September 17, 2018, https://www.theguardian.com/commentisfree/2018/sep/17/amazon-warehouse-bernie-sanders.
2. Zoe Williams, "Do You Want to Feel Really Good This Christmas? Boycott Amazon," *Guardian*, December 3, 2019, https://www.theguardian.com/technology/shortcuts/2019/dec/03/boycott-amazon-christmas-workers-ceo-jeff-bezos.
3. André Spicer, "Amazon's 'Worker Cage' Has Been Dropped, But Its Staff Are Not Free," *Guardian*, September 14, 2018, https://www.theguardian.com/commentisfree/2018/sep/14/amazon-worker-cage-staff.
4. Michael Sainato, "'Go Back to Work': Outcry over Deaths on Amazon Warehouse Floor," *Guardian*, October 18, 2019, https://www.theguardian.com/technology/2019/oct/17/amazon-warehouse-worker-deaths.
5. Karl Marx, *The Economic and Philosophical Manuscripts of 1844*, ed. Dirk J. Struik, trans. Martin Milligan (New York: International Publishers, 1964), 111, 108, 65.
6. Ibid., 110.
7. Berardi, *The Soul at Work*, 115.
8. Ibid., 23.
9. Ibid., 74.
10. Suarez-Villa, *Technocapitalism*, 30–3.
11. Berardi, *The Soul at Work*, 78.
12. Ibid., 79.
13. Ibid., 83.
14. Ibid., 81, 80.
15. Berardi, *And*, 110.
16. Berardi, *The Soul at Work*, 22.
17. Ibid., 21, 115, 133.
18. Ibid., 115.
19. Ibid., 80.
20. See the DoorDash website: https://www.doordash.com/dasher/signup/?source=dx_signup_help_header.
21. Richard Schacht, *Alienation* (New York: Doubleday & Company, Inc., 1971).

22 Jana Costas and Peter Fleming, "Beyond Dis-Identification: A Discursive Approach to Self-Alienation in Contemporary Organizations," *Human Relations* 62, no. 3 (2009): 353–78, 365, 368, 366.
23 Arendt, *The Human Condition*, 126.
24 Ibid., 322.
25 Suarez-Villa, *Technocapitalism*, 35.
26 Phil Daoust, "The New Rules of Eating al desko," *Guardian*, January 10, 2019, https://www.theguardian.com/food/2019/jan/10/the-new-rules-of-eating-al-desko.
27 Berardi, *The Soul at Work*, 24.

In the Desert

1 Camus, *The Myth of Sisyphus and Other Essays*, v.
2 Ibid., 12.
3 Arendt, *The Promise of Politics*, 202.

The Iron Band of Technology

1 Casey Newton, "The Trauma Floor: The Secret Lives of Facebook Moderators in America," *The Verge*, February 25, 2019, https://www.theverge.com/2019/2/25/18229714/cognizant-facebook-content-moderator-interviews-trauma-working-conditions-arizona.
2 Andrew Marantz, "The Dark Side of Techno-Utopianism," *New Yorker*, September 30, 2019, https://www.newyorker.com/magazine/2019/09/30/the-dark-side-of-techno-utopianism.
3 Ibid.
4 Berardi, *And*, 12, 14–18, 13, 23.
5 Ibid., 18, 21–3, 23.
6 Ibid., 18.
7 Zygmunt Bauman and Thomas Leoncini, *Born Liquid: Transformations in the Third Millennium* (Cambridge, UK: Polity Press, 2019), 65, 66.
8 Berardi, *And*, 70.
9 Ibid., 67–8.
10 Ibid., 12, 296–7, 110.

11 With the exception of "Rent-a-Family," a largely Japanese industry, these examples were taken from a UK government report: "A Connected Society: A Strategy for Tackling Loneliness—Laying the Foundation for Change," Department for Digital, Culture, Media and Sport, London, October 2018, https://assets.publishing.service.gov.uk/government/uploads/system/uploads/attachment_data/file/750909/6.4882_DCMS_Loneliness_Strategy_web_Update.pdf.
12 Arendt, *The Promise of Politics*, 202, 203.

Social Failure

1 Anna Fifield, "Cleaning Up after the Dead," *Washington Post*, January 24, 2018, https://www.washingtonpost.com/news/world/wp/2018/01/24/feature/so-many-japanese-people-die-alone-theres-a-whole-industry-devoted-to-cleaning-up-after-them/.
2 Eleanor Ainge Roy, "New Zealand University Student Lay Dead in Room for Nearly Two Months," *Guardian*, 25 September, 2019, https://www.theguardian.com/world/2019/sep/25/new-zealand-university-student-lay-dead-in-room-for-nearly-two-months.
3 Arendt, *The Promise of Politics*, 201.
4 Sachiko Horiguchi, "*Hikikomori:* How Private Isolation Caught the Public Eye," in *A Sociology of Japanese Youth: From Returnees to NEETs*, ed. Roger Goodman, Yuki Imoto and Tuukka Toivonen (New York: Routledge), 127.
5 A recent government survey estimated the numbers were slightly higher among men and women aged forty to sixty-four than fifteen to thirty-nine. See "613,000 in Japan Aged 40 to 64 Are Recluses, Says First Government Survey of Hikikomori," *Japan Times*, March 29, 2019, https://www.japantimes.co.jp/news/2019/03/29/national/613000-japan-aged-40-64-recluses-says-first-government-survey-hikikomori/.
6 Karin Amamiya, "'*Ikizurasa' nitsuite: hinkon, aidentiti, nashyonarizumu*" (Tokyo: Kobunsha shinsho), quoted in Anne Allison, *Precarious Japan* (Durham: Duke University Press, 2013), 67.
7 Horiguchi, "*Hikikomori*: How Private Isolation Caught the Public Eye," 130.
8 Berardi, *And*, 104–5.
9 Allison, *Precarious Japan*, 73.
10 Horiguchi, "*Hikikomori:* How Private Isolation Caught the Public Eye," 127–8.

11 Weiyi Kai and Simone Landon, "Attacks by White Extremists Are Growing. So Are Their Connections," *New York Times*, April 3, 2019, https://www.nytimes.com/interactive/2019/04/03/world/white-extremist-terrorism-christchurch.html.

12 Elliot Rodger, "My Twisted World: The Story of Elliot Rodger," accessed June 23, 2021, https://www.documentcloud.org/documents/1173808-elliot-rodger-manifesto.html.

13 "George Sodini's Blog: Full Text by Alleged Gym Shooter," *ABC News*, August 5, 2009, https://abcnews.go.com/US/story?id=8258001&page=1.

Pandemic Pause

1 Cecilia Kang, "The Humble Phone Call Has Made a Comeback," *New York Times*, April 9, 2020, https://www.nytimes.com/2020/04/09/technology/phone-calls-voice-virus.html.

2 Greta Anderson, "Feeling Shortchanged," *Inside Higher Ed*, April 13, 2020, https://www.insidehighered.com/news/2020/04/13/students-say-online-classes-arent-what-they-paid.

3 Masha Gessen, "How the Coronavirus Pandemic Has Shattered the Myth of College in America," *New Yorker*, April 28, 2020, https://www.newyorker.com/news/us-journal/how-the-coronavirus-pandemic-has-shattered-the-myth-of-college-in-america?utm_source=onsite-share&utm_medium=email&utm_campaign=onsite-share&utm_brand=the-new-yorker.

4 At the time of writing, a vaccine was still many months away. Now we know that it wasn't the panacea the world hoped it would be, and gave rise to antisocial forces that render a social distancing mandate relatively innocuous by comparison.

To Belong

1 A. K. Ramanujan, *Journeys: A Poet's Diary*, ed. Krishna Ramanujan and Guillermo Rodriguez (Gurgaon: Hamish Hamilton/Penguin), quoted in David Shulman, "Waiting for the Perfect Word," *The New York Review of Books*, September 26, 2019, Vol. LXVI, Number 14, p. 82. Italics added.

2 Koji Tsukino, quoted in Anne Allison, *Precarious Japan*, 3.

3 Arendt, *The Origins of Totalitarianism*, 296.

4 Ibid., 296.

5 Ibid., 302.
6 Ibid.

Proximity

1 Jenny Erpenbeck, *Go, Went, Gone*, trans. Susan Bernofsky (New York: New Directions Books, 2017), 121–2.
2 Vivian Gornick, "Letter from Greenwich Village," in *The Best American Essays 2014*, ed. John Jeremiah Sullivan (New York: Houghton Mifflin Harcourt, 2014), 49–65, 65.

Distance

1 Georg Simmel, *On Individuality and Social Forms*, ed. Donald N. Levine (Chicago: University of Chicago Press, 1971), 335.
2 Atul Gawande, *On Being Mortal: Medicine and What Matters in the End* (Doubleday Canada, 2014), 15.
3 Ibid., 20.
4 Simmel, *On Individuality and Social Forms*, 324.
5 Ibid., 333.
6 de Beauvoir, *The Ethics of Ambiguity*, 91.
7 Barthes, *How to Live Together*, 132.

In the Neighborhood

1 Jane Jacobs, *The Death and Life of Great American Cities*, Vintage Books Edition (New York: Vintage Books, 1992), 55, 62, 64.
2 Ibid., 56.
3 Ibid., 59–60, 61.
4 Ibid., 68, 69, 70.
5 Ibid., 116.
6 Jane Jacobs, *Dark Age Ahead* (Toronto: Vintage Canada, 2004), 3–4.

At the Café

1 Stein, *Philosophy of Psychology and the Humanities*, 145.
2 Simmel, *On Individuality and Social Forms*, 329.

At the Market

1 Berardi, *The Soul at Work*, 80.

Care

1 Campbell Robertson and Robert Gebeloff, "How Millions of Women Became the Most Essential Workers in America," *New York Times*, April 18, 2020, https://www.nytimes.com/2020/04/18/us/coronavirus-women-essential-workers.html
2 Adam Carter, "Military Report Reveals What Sector Has Long Known: Ontario's Nursing Homes Are in Trouble," *CBC*, May 27, 2020, https://www.cbc.ca/news/canada/toronto/military-long-term-care-home-report-covid-ontario-1.5585844.
3 Julie Ireton, "Covid-19: Majority of Region's Long-Term Care Deaths Occurred in For-Profit Homes," *CBC News*, June 10, 2020, https://www.cbc.ca/news/canada/ottawa/for-profit-nursing-homes-83-percent-of-covid-deaths-eastern-ontario-1.5604880.
4 Simone Weil, *The Need for Roots: Prelude to a Declaration of Duties towards Mankind*, trans. Arthur Wills (New York: Routledge, 2002), 3–5.

Friendship

1 Simone Weil, *Oppression and Liberty*, trans. Arthur Wills and John Petrie (New York: Routledge, 2001), 94, 79, 81, 79.
2 Plato, *Symposium*, 53, note 79.
3 Plato, *Symposium*, 57.
4 Morrison, *Beloved*, 116.

Love

1. Michel de Montaigne, *Essays*, trans. J. M. Cohen (London: Penguin Books, 1993), 97.
2. Morrison, *Beloved*, 213.

The Join

1. Morrison, *Beloved*, 272–3.

Witness

1. Sheila Heti, "My Life Is a Joke," *New Yorker*, May 11, 2015, https://www.newyorker.com/magazine/2015/05/11/my-life-is-a-joke.
2. Ibid.

BIBLIOGRAPHY

Abbott, Jack Henry. *In the Belly of the Beast: Letters from Prison*. New York: Random House, 1981.

ABC News. "George Sodini's Blog: Full Text by Alleged Gym Shooter." August 5, 2009. https://abcnews.go.com/US/story?id=8258001&page=1.

Allison, Anne. *Precarious Japan*. Durham: Duke University Press, 2013.

Amamiya, Karin, and Kayano Toshihito. *"Ikizurasa" nitsuite: hinkon, aidentiti, nashyonarizumu*. Tokyo: Kobunsha shinsho, 2008.

Anderson, Greta. "Feeling Shortchanged." *Inside Higher Ed*, April 13, 2020. https://www.insidehighered.com/news/2020/04/13/students-say-online-classes-arent-what-they-paid.

Appiah, Kwame Anthony. *The Lies That Bind: Rethinking Identity*. New York: Liveright Publishing Co., 2018.

Arendt, Hannah. *The Human Condition*. Chicago: University of Chicago Press, 1958.

Arendt, Hannah. *The Life of the Mind*. One-volume ed. New York: Harcourt, Inc, 1971.

Arendt, Hannah. *The Origins of Totalitarianism*. Rev. ed. New York: Harcourt Brace & Company, 1973.

Arendt, Hannah. *The Promise of Politics*. Edited by Jerome Kohn. New York: Schocken Books, 2005.

Barrett, Michèle, and Mary McIntosh. *The Anti-Social Family*. New York: Verso Press, 2015.

Barthes, Roland. *How to Live Together: Novelistic Simulations of Some Everyday Spaces*. Translated by Kate Briggs. New York: Columbia University Press, 2013.

Bauman, Zygmunt. *Community: Seeking Safety in an Insecure World*. Oxford: Polity Press, 2001.

Bauman, Zygmunt, and Thomas Leoncini. *Born Liquid: Transformations in the Third Millennium*. Cambridge, UK: Polity Press, 2019.

BBC News. "Bolivian Mennonites Jailed for Serial Rapes." August 26, 2011. https://www.bbc.com/news/world-latin-america-14688458.

BBC Sounds: In Our Time. "The Philosophy of Solitude." Thomas Morris, producer. Melvyn Bragg with Simon Blackburn, John Haldane, and Melissa Lane. June 19, 2014. https://www.bbc.co.uk/sounds/play/b046ntnz.

BIBLIOGRAPHY 189

Beauvoir, Simone de. *The Ethics of Ambiguity*. Translated by Bernard Frechtman. New York: Citadel Press, 1976.

Franco "Bifo" Berardi. *And: Phenomenology of the End*. South Pasadena, CA: Semiotext(e), 2015.

Berardi, Franco "Bifo." *The Soul at Work: From Alienation to Autonomy*. Translated by Francesca Cadel and Giuseppina Mecchia. South Pasadena, CA: Semiotext(e), 2009.

Blackburn, Simon, John Haldane and Melissa Lane. "The Philosophy of Solitude." By Thomas Morris Audio. *BBC Sounds: In Our Time*. June 19, 2014. https://www.bbc.co.uk/sounds/play/b046ntnz.

Bloodworth, James. "I Worked in an Amazon Warehouse: Bernie Sanders Is Right to Target Them." *Guardian*, September 17, 2018. https://www.theguardian.com/commentisfree/2018/sep/17/amazon-warehouse-bernie-sanders.

Bolick, Kate. *Spinster*. New York: Broadway Books, 2016.

Bowlby, John. *Attachment and Loss, Vol. 1: Attachment*. New York: Basic Books, 1969.

Brake, Elizabeth. *Minimizing Marriage: Marriage, Morality, and the Law*. Oxford: Oxford University Press, 2012.

Buber, Martin. *Between Man and Man*. Translated by Ronald Gregor-Smith. New York: Routledge, 2002.

Cacioppo, John T., and William Patrick. *Loneliness: Human Nature and the Need for Social Connection*. New York: W.W. Norton & Company, 2008.

Calcagno, Antonio. *Lived Experience from the Inside Out: Social and Political Philosophy in Edith Stein*. Pittsburgh, PA: Duquesne University Press, 2014.

Camus, Albert. *The Myth of Sisyphus and Other Essays*. Translated by Justin O'Brien. New York: Vintage Books, 1991.

Camus, Albert. "The Myth of Sisyphus." In *The Myth of Sisyphus and Other Essays*, translated by Justin O'Brien, 119–23. New York: Vintage International, 1991.

Camus, Albert. *The Rebel: An Essay on Man in Revolt*. Translated by Anthony Bower. New York: Vintage Books, 1976.

Card, Claudia. "Against Marriage and Motherhood." *Hypatia* 11, no. 3 (1996): 1–23.

Carter, Adam. "Military Report Reveals What Sector Has Long Known: Ontario's Nursing Homes Are in Trouble." *CBC*, May 27, 2020. https://www.cbc.ca/news/canada/toronto/military-long-term-care-home-report-covid-ontario-1.5585844.

Chopin, Kate. *The Awakening and Selected Stories*. New York: Penguin Books, 1984.

CIA. KUBARK Counterintelligence Interrogation. 1963. Quoted in Lisa Guenther. *Solitary Confinement: Social Death and Its Afterlives*. Minneapolis: University of Minnesota Press, 2013.

Costas, Jana, and Peter Fleming. "Beyond Dis-Identification: A Discursive Approach to Self-Alienation in Contemporary Organizations." *Human Relations* 62, no. 3 (2009): 353–78.

Daoust, Phil. "The New Rules of Eating Al Desko." *Guardian*, January 10, 2019. https://www.theguardian.com/food/2019/jan/10/the-new-rules-of-eating-al-desko.

Department for Digital, Culture, Media, and Sport. "A Connected Society: A Strategy for Tackling Loneliness—Laying the Foundation for Change." PDF file. Department for Digital, Culture, Media, Sport. London, October 2018. https://assets.publishing.service.gov.uk/government/uploads/system/uploads/attachment_data/file750909/6.4882_DCMS_Loneliness_Strategy_web_Update.pdf.

DePaulo, Bella. *How We Live Now: Redefining Home and Family in the 21st Century*. New York: Atria Books, 2015.

DePaulo, Bella. "Single People Aren't to Blame for the Loneliness Epidemic." *The Atlantic: Family*. August 28, 2018. https://www.theatlantic.com/family/archive/2018/08/single-people-arent-to-blame-for-the-loneliness-epidemic/568786/.

DePaulo, Bella. "Why Are You Still Single?: Here's the Best Way to Answer." *Living Single* (blog). *Psychology Today*. July 27, 2019. https://www.psychologytoday.com/ca/blog/living-single/201907/why-are-you-single-here-are-some-my-favorite-answers.

Doordash. "Sign Up." (website). https://www.doordash.com/dasher/signup/?source=dx_signup_help_header.

Dumm, Thomas. *Loneliness as a Way of Life*. Cambridge, MA: Harvard University Press, 2010.

Emerson, Ralph Waldo. *Self-Reliance*. PDF file. 1841. https://math.dartmouth.edu/~doyle/docs/self/self.pdf.

Enns, Diane. "The Other L Word." Interview by Joe Gelonesi. *Philosophers Zone*. ABC, April 23, 2017. Audio, 25:31. https://www.abc.net.au/radionational/programs/philosopherszone/the-other-l-word-loneliness/8454692.

Epictetus. "Enchiridion." In *Epictetus: Discourses and Selected Writings*, translated by Robert Dobbin, 219–45. London: Penguin Books, 2008.

Erpenbeck, Jenny. *Go, Went, Gone*. Translated by Susan Bernofsky. New York: New Directions Books, 2017.

Esposito, Roberto. *Terms of the Political: Community, Immunity, Biopolitics*. Translated by Rhiannon Noel Welch. New York: Fordham University Press, 2013.

Fifeld, Anna. "Cleaning Up after the Dead." *Washington Post*, January 24, 2018. https://www.washingtonpost.com/news/world/wp/2018/01/24/feature/so-many-japanese-people-die-alone-theres-a-whole-industry-devoted-to-cleaning-up-after-them/.

Finkel, Michael. "Into the Woods: How One Man Survived Alone in the Wilderness for 27 Years." *Guardian*, March 15, 2017. https://www.theguardian.com/news/2017/mar/15/stranger-in-the-woods-christopher-knight-hermit-maine.

Finkel, Michael. "The Strange and Curious Tale of the Last True Hermit." *GQ*, August 5, 2014. https://www.gq.com/story/the-last-true-hermit.

Freud, Sigmund. "The Uncanny" (1919). In *The Standard Edition of the Complete Psychological Works of Sigmund Freud Volume XVII (1917–1919): An Infantile Neurosis and Other Works*, edited and translated by James Strachey, 217–56. London: Vintage Books, 2001.

Friedman-Rudovsky, Jean. "The Ghost Rapes of Bolivia." *Vice*, December 22, 2013. https://www.vice.com/en_ca/article/4w7gqj/the-ghost-rapes-of-bolivia-000300-v20n8.

Friedman-Rudovsky, Jean. "The Verdict in Bolivia's Shocking Case of the Mennonite Rapes." *Time*, August 17, 2011. http://content.time.com/time/world/article/0,8599,2087711,00.html.

Fromm, Erich. *The Art of Loving*. New York: Harper & Row Publishers, 1956.

Fromm-Reichmann, Frieda. "Loneliness." *Psychiatry* 22, no. 1 (1959): 1–15.

Gawande, Atul. "Hellhole." *New Yorker*, March 30, 2009. https://www.newyorker.com/magazine/2009/03/30/hellhole.

Gawande, Atul. *On Being Mortal: Medicine and What Matters in the End*. Toronto: Doubleday Canada, 2014.

Gessen, Masha. "How the Coronavirus Pandemic Has Shattered the Myth of College in America." *New Yorker*, April 28, 2020. https://www.newyorker.com/news/us-journal/how-the-coronavirus-pandemic-has-shattered-the-myth-of-college-in-america?utm_source=onsite-share&utm_medium=email&utm_campaign=onsite-share&utm_brand=the-new-yorker.

Gornick, Vivian. "Letter from Greenwich Village." In *The Best American Essays 2014*, edited by John Jeremiah Sullivan, 49–65. New York: Houghton Mifflin Harcourt, 2014.

Green, Hannah. *I Never Promised You a Rose Garden: A Novel*. New York: St. Martin's Press, 1964.

Guenther, Lisa. *Solitary Confinement: Social Death and Its Afterlives*. Minneapolis: University of Minnesota Press, 2013.

Hartog, Joseph, Ralph Audy, and Yehudi A. Cohen. *The Anatomy of Loneliness*. New York: International Universities Press, 1980.

Heti, Sheila. "My Life Is a Joke." *New Yorker*, May 11, 2015. https://www.newyorker.com/magazine/2015/05/11/my-life-is-a-joke.

Hinkle, Lawrence E., and Harold G. Wolff. *Communist Interrogation and Indoctrination of "Enemies of the State."* American Medical Association, 1956.

Horiguchi, Sachiko. "*Hikikomori*: How Private Isolation Caught the Public Eye." In *A Sociology of Japanese Youth: From Returnees to NEETs*, edited by Roger Goodman, Yuki Imoto, and Tuukka Toivonen, 122–38. New York: Routledge, 2012.

Ireton, Julie. "COVID-19: Majority of Region's Long-Term Care Deaths Occurred in for-Profit Homes." *CBC NEWS*, June 10, 2020. https://www.cbc.ca/news/canada/ottawa/for-profit-nursing-homes-83-percent-of-covid-deaths-eastern-ontario-1.5604880.

Jacobs, Jane. *Dark Age Ahead*. Toronto: Vintage Canada, 2004.

Jacobs, Jane. *The Death and Life of Great American Cities*. New York: Vintage Books, 1992.

Kafka, Franz. *Metamorphosis and Other Stories*. Translated by Michael Hofmann. London: Penguin Books, 2007.

Kai, Weiyi, and Simone Landon. "Attacks by White Extremists Are Growing. So Are Their Connections." *New York Times*, April 3, 2019. https://www.nytimes.com/interactive/2019/04/03/world/white-extremist-terrorism-christchurch.html.

Kang, Cecilia. "The Humble Phone Call Has Made a Comeback." *New York Times*, April 9, 2020. https://www.nytimes.com/2020/04/09/technology/phone-calls-voice-virus.html.

Kennedy, Maev. "Loo with a View." *Guardian*, December 4, 2003. https://www.theguardian.com/uk/2003/dec/04/arts.artsnews.

Klein, Melanie. "On the Sense of Loneliness." In *Envy and Gratitude and Other Works 1946–1963*, edited by Roger Money-Kyrle, Vol. III, 300–13. New York: The Free Press, 1975.

Klinenberg, Eric. *Going Solo*. London: Penguin Books, 2013.

Korda, Marissa. "The Loneliness Project." http://thelonelinessproject.org/.

Laing, Olivia. *The Lonely City*. London: Picador, 2016.

Maitland, Sara. *How to Be Alone*. London: Macmillan Publishers, 2014.

Maitland, Sara. "Savour Solitude—It Is Not the Same as Loneliness." *Guardian*, May 17, 2020. https://www.theguardian.com/society/2020/may/17/sara-maitland-savour-solitude-it-is-not-the-same-as-loneliness.

Marantz, Andrew. "The Dark Side of Techno-Utopianism." *New Yorker*, September 30, 2019. https://www.newyorker.com/magazine/2019/09/30/the-dark-side-of-techno-utopianism.

Marx, Karl. *The Economic and Philosophical Manuscripts of 1844*. Edited by Dirk J. Struik. Translated by Martin Milligan. New York: International Publishers, 1964.

May, Rollo. *Man's Search for Himself*. New York: W.W. Norton & Company, 1953.

Melandri, Lea. *Love and Violence: The Vexatious Factors of Civilization*. Translated by Antonio Calcagno. Albany: SUNY Press, 2019.

Monbiot, George. "The Age of Loneliness Is Killing Us." *Guardian*, October 14, 2014. https://www.theguardian.com/commentisfree/2014/oct/14/age-of-loneliness-killing-us.

Montaigne, Michel de. "Of Solitude." In *Essays of Michel de Montaigne*, edited by William Hazlitt. Translated by Charles Cotton. Project Gutenberg, 1877. https://www.gutenberg.org/files/3600/3600-h/3600-h.htm.

Montaigne, Michel de. *Essays*. Translated by J. M. Cohen. London: Penguin Books, 1993.

Morrison, Toni. *Beloved*. New York: Plume, 1987.

Moustakas, Clark E. *Loneliness*. N.p.: Pickle Partners Publishing, 2016. Kindle.

Newton, Casey. "The Trauma Floor: The Secret Lives of Facebook Moderators in America." *The Verge*, February 25, 2019. https://www.theverge.com

BIBLIOGRAPHY

/2019/2/25/18229714/cognizant-facebook-content-moderator-interviews-trauma-working-conditions-arizona.

Nietzsche, Friedrich. *Twilight of the Idol*. Translated by Duncan Large. Oxford: Oxford University Press, 1998.

Paz, Octavio. *The Labyrinth of Solitude*. Translated by Lysander Kemp, Yara Milos, and Rachel Phillips Belash. New York: Grove Press, 1985.

Peplau, Letitia Anne, and Daniel Perlman. *Loneliness: A Sourcebook of Current Theory, Research and Therapy*. New York: John Wiley & Sons, 1982.

Pinker, Susan. *The Village Effect: How Face-to-Face Contact Can Make Us Healthier, Happier, and Smarter*. Toronto: Vintage Canada, 2015.

Plato. *Symposium*. Translated by Alexander Nehamas and Paul Woodruff. Indianapolis: Hackett Publishing Co., 1989.

Rahim, Sameer. "Doris Lessing: In Her Own Words." *The Telegraph*, November 17, 2013. https://www.telegraph.co.uk/culture/books/booknews/10455645/Doris-Lessing-in-her-own-words.html.

Ramanujan, A. K. *Journeys: A Poet's Diary*. Edited by Krishna Ramanujan and Guillermo Rodriguez. Gurgaon: Hamish Hamilton, 2019.

Robertson, Campbell and Robert Gebeloff. "How Millions of Women Became the Most Essential Workers in America." *New York Times*, April 18, 2020. https://www.nytimes.com/2020/04/18/us/coronavirus-women-essential-workers.html.

Rodger, Elliot. "My Twisted World: The Story of Elliot Roger." PDF file. https://www.documentcloud.org/documents/1173808-elliot-rodger-manifesto.html.

Rouner, Leroy S., ed. *Loneliness*. Notre Dame, IN: University of Notre Dame Press, 1998.

Roy, Eleanor Ainge. "New Zealand University Student Lay Dead in Room for Nearly Two Months." *Guardian*, September 25, 2019. https://www.theguardian.com/world/2019/sep/25/new-zealand-university-student-lay-dead-in-room-for-nearly-two-months.

Ryan, Denise. "Novelist Says Loneliness Is a 'Very Privileged' Thing." *Vancouver Sun*, February 24, 2017. https://vancouversun.com/entertainment/books/novelist-says-lonesomeness-a-very-privileged-thing.

Sagan, Olivia, and Eric Miller, eds. *Narratives of Loneliness: Multidisciplinary Perspectives from the 21st Century*. New York: Rutledge, 2017.

Sainato, Michael. "'Go Back to Work': Outcry over Deaths on Amazon Warehouse Floor." *Guardian*, October 18, 2019. https://www.theguardian.com/technology/2019/oct/17/amazon-warehouse-worker-deaths.

Salomé, Lou. *Nietzsche*. Translated by Siegfried Mandel. Chicago: University of Illinois Press, 2001.

Sarton, May. *Journal of a Solitude*. New York: W.W. Norton & Company, 1973.

Sartre, Jean-Paul. *Being and Nothingness*. Translated by Hazel E. Barnes. New York: Washington Square Press, 1992.

Sartre, Jean-Paul. "Freedom and Responsibility." In *Essays in Existentialism*, edited by Wade Baskin, 63–8. New York: Citadel Press, 1993.

Sartre, Jean-Paul. "No Exit." In *No Exit and Three Other Plays*, translated by S. Gilbert. New York: Vintage International Edition, 1989.
Sartre, Jean-Paul. "The Humanism of Existentialism." In *Essays in Existentialism*. New York: Citadel Press, 1993.
Schacht, Richard. *Alienation*. New York: Doubleday, 1971.
Schipani, Andres. "'The Work of the Devil': Crime in a Remote Religious Community." *Guardian*, September 10, 2009. https://www.theguardian.com/world/2009/sep/10/mennonites-rape-bolivia.
Schulman, David. "Waiting for the Perfect World." *New York Review of Books* 66, no. 14 (September 26, 2019).
Schulz, Kathryn. "The Moral Judgements of Henry David Thoreau." *New Yorker*, October 19, 2015. https://www.newyorker.com/magazine/2015/10/19/pond-scum.
Sen, Amartya. *Identity and Violence: The Illusion of Destiny*. New York: Penguin Books, 2006.
Shulevitz, Judith. "The Lethality of Loneliness." *New Republic*, May 13, 2013. https://newrepublic.com/article113176/science-loneliness-how-isolation-can-kill-you.
Simmel, Georg. *On Individuality and Social Forms*. Edited by Donald N. Levine. Chicago: University of Chicago Press, 1971.
Singer, Irving. "Appraisal and Bestowal." In *The Nature of Love, Vol. I: Plato to Luther*. 2nd ed., 3–22. Chicago: University of Chicago Press, 1984.
"Six Things You Need to Know about Monica Bonvicini." *Phaidon*. https://ca.phaidon.com/agenda/art/articles/2014/june/17/six-things-you-need-to-know-about-monica-bonvicini/.
Smith, Dana G. "Neuroscientists Make a Case against Solitary Confinement." *Scientific American*, November 9, 2018. https://www.scientificamerican.com/article/neuroscientists-make-a-case-against-solitary-confinement/.
Snell, K. D. M. "The Rise of Living Alone and Loneliness in History." *Social History* 42, no. 1 (2017): 2–28.
Sontag, Susan. "Pilgrimage." In *Debriefing: Collected Stories*, edited by Benjamin Taylor, 1–30. New York: Farrar, Straus and Giroux, 2017.
Spicer, André. "Amazon's 'Worker Cage' Has Been Dropped, But Its Staff Are Not Free." *Guardian*, September 14, 2018. https://www.theguardian.com/commentisfree/2018/sep/14/amazon-worker-cage-staff.
Stein, Edith. *On the Problem of Empathy*. Translated by Waltraut Stein. Washington, DC: ICS Publications, 1989.
Stein, Edith. *Philosophy of Psychology and the Humanities*. Edited by Marianne Sawicki. Translated by Mary Catharine Baseheart and Marianne Sawicki. Washington, DC: ICS Publications, 2000.
Stevens, Anthony. "Anthony Storr." *Guardian*, March 20, 2001. https://www.theguardian.com/news/2001/mar/20/guardianobituaries.highereducation.
Storr, Anthony. *Solitude: A Return to the Self*. New York: Free Press, 1988.
Stuck, Franz von. *Sisyphus*. 1920. Oil on Canvas. Galerie Ritthaler, München. https://fineartamerica.com/featured/sisyphus-franz-von-stuck.html.

BIBLIOGRAPHY

Suarez-Villa, Luis. *Technocapitalism: A Critical Perspective on Technological Innovation and Corporatism.* Philadelphia: Temple University Press, 2009.

Sullivan, Harry Stack. *The Interpersonal Theory of Psychiatry.* New York: W. W. Norton & Company, 1953.

Svendsen, Lars. *A Philosophy of Loneliness.* London: Reaktion Books, 2017.

Thoreau, Henry David. *Walden.* Edited by Stephen Fender. New York: Oxford University Press, 1977.

Tillich, Paul. "Loneliness and Solitude." In *The Anatomy of Loneliness*, edited by Joseph Hartog, J. Ralph Audy, and Yehudi A Cohen, 547–53. New York: International Universities Press, 1980.

Tönnies, Ferdinand. *Community and Society.* Translated by Charles P. Loomis. New York: Harper & Row, 1963.

Traister, Rebecca. *All the Single Ladies.* New York: Simon & Schuster, 2016.

Turkle, Sherry. *Alone Together: Why We Expect More from Technology and Less from Each Other.* New York: Basic Books, 2011.

Turkle, Sherry. "Connected, But Alone." February 2012. TED video. https://www.ted.com/talks/sherry_turkle_connected_but_alone?language=en.

Vora, Shivaji. "How Neil Patrick Harris and David Burtka Spend Their Sundays." *New York Times*, June 14, 2019. https://www.nytimes.com/2019/06/14/nyregion/neil-patrick-harris-david-burtka.html?searchResultPosition=1.

"Vulnerable." *Online Etymology Dictionary.* https://www.etymonline.com/word/vulnerable.

Wang, Lulu, dir. *The Farewell.* Ray Productions, 2019. https://www.imdb.com/title/tt8637428/.

Weil, Simone. *The Need for Roots: Prelude to a Declaration of Duties towards Mankind.* Translated by Arthur Wills. New York: Routledge, 2002.

Weil, Simone. *Oppression and Liberty.* Translated by Arthur Wills and John Petrie. New York: Routledge, 2001.

Weiss, Robert S. *Loneliness: The Experience of Emotional and Social Isolation.* Cambridge, MA: MIT Press, 1975.

Wellesley, Mary. "The Life of the Anchoress." *Discovering Literature: Medieval*, March 13, 2018. https://www.bl.uk/medieval-literature/articles/the-life-of-the-anchoress.

White, Emily. *Lonely: Learning to Live with Solitude.* Toronto: McClelland & Steward, 2010.

Williams, Tennessee. *Orpheus Descending.* PDF file. 1958. http://www.newmoontheatre.org/uploads/2/1/7/6/21764846/orpheus_edit_12-3.pdf.

Williams, Zoe. "Do You Want to Feel Really Good This Christmas? Boycott Amazon." *Guardian*, December 3, 2019. https://www.theguardian.com/technology/shortcuts/2019/dec/03/boycott-amazon-christmas-workers-ceo-jeff-bezos.

Willis, Paul. "This Reclusive Life: What I Learned about Solitude from My Time with Hermits." *Guardian*, October 6, 2017. https://www.theguardian.com/us-news/2017/oct/06/hermits-solitude-wilderness-new-mexico.

Woolf, Virginia. *A Room of One's Own; Three Guineas*. Edited by Michèle Barrett. New York: Penguin Books, 1993.
Woolf, Virginia. "On Being Ill." In *Selected Essays*, edited by David Bradshaw, 101–10. Oxford: Oxford University Press, 2008.
Woolf, Virginia. *To the Lighthouse*. London: Grafton Books, 1977.
Zilboorg, Gregory. "Loneliness." *Atlantic Monthly*, January 1938, 45–54.
Zuboff, Shoshana. "Big Other: Surveillance Capitalism and the Prospects of an Information Civilization." *Journal of Information Technology* 30, no. 1 (2015): 75–89. https://doi.org/10.1057/jit.2015.5.

INDEX

abandonment 33, 67, 75
Abbott, Jack Henry 44
absurdity 39, 73, 79, 112, 113
age of loneliness 17
alienation 5, 25, 31–2, 40, 69, 71, 100–5, 111–14
aloneness 4, 6, 8–10, 25, 33–41, 48–51, 57, 60–2
alone together 59–62
Alone Together: Why We Expect More from Technology and Less from Each Other 59–62
Amamiya, Karin 125
amatonormativity 77
Amazon 100, 101
anchoress 47
anchorite 47
Ancrene Wisse 47
Anderson, Terry 43
antisocial family 82–8. See also family
The Anti-Social Family 87
anxiety 8, 9, 17, 35, 39, 50, 54, 109, 110
Appiah, Kwame Anthony 93
Arendt, Hannah 26–8, 53, 60, 66–70, 96, 105, 111, 113,
116, 122, 124–5, 127, 136, 139–40, 155
The Art of Loving 76
The Awakening 82

Barrett, Michèle 73, 85–7
Barthes, Roland 66, 83, 84, 146, 154
Bauman, Zygmunt 94–6, 121
Beauvoir, Simone de 38, 39, 146
Being Mortal 145
belonging 138–40
Beloved 22, 163, 165, 166
Berardi, Franco 69, 93, 100–3, 105, 107, 110, 119–22, 126, 156
Blackburn, Simon 46
Bonvicini, Monica 3
Brake, Elizabeth 77, 78
Buber, Martin 60

Cacioppo, John T. 17–20, 26
café life 151–4
Camus, Albert 37–9, 112, 113
capitalism 68–70, 101–2, 158
    digital 70, 120
    semio– 69
    surveillance 70

techno– 69–70, 133–4
capitalist absolutism 123
care 73, 87, 150, 157–60, 164–5
Chopin, Kate 82
chronic loneliness 4, 12, 16
cognitariat 101–3
cognitive labor 102, 103
commodification 70, 102, 108
common sense 67, 155, 156
community 12–13, 60, 89–98, 138, 139, 147
Community and Society 92
compulsory coupledom 77, 88
conjunctive 60, 119–20
connective 120, 121
conviviality 155–6
Covid-19 51, 131–7, 159, 160
craving, loneliness as 22, 23, 26, 31, 87, 164
creativity 52–3, 107–8

death 10, 34–5, 39, 44, 60–1, 75, 97, 157, 160
  living 43
The Death and Life of Great American Cities 147
death row 44
DePaulo, Bella 78
desert 42, 46, 48, 68, 70, 102, 112–15, 123–5
desire 16–17, 23–6, 31, 55, 57, 93–5, 122, 141, 144, 165
distance 66, 144–6
"Don't Miss a Sec" 3
Dumm, Thomas 4

The Economic and Philosophic Manuscripts of 1844 100
egoism *à deux* 76
Eliot, George 93
Emerson, Ralph Waldo 40, 41
emotional loneliness 15–16
Epictetus 17
eros in everyday life 102, 107, 156
Erpenbeck, Jenny 141
Esposito, Roberto 94
estrangement 32, 37
The Ethics of Ambiguity 38
existentialism 36–40

family 12, 18, 66, 72, 77. *See also* antisocial family
The Farewell 98
Finkel, Michael 45
Freud, Sigmund 8
friendship 51–2, 76, 77, 122, 123, 161–3
Fromm, Erich 69, 76
Fromm-Reichmann, Frieda 14, 24–8, 40, 48, 49, 127

Gawande, Atul 145
Gessen, Masha 135
"ghost rapes" 90
Go, Went, Gone 141
Graves, Anthony 44
grief 9–10, 25, 29–30
Guardian 14

Haldane, John 46
hermits 45, 46, 48
Heti, Sheila 168

INDEX

hikikomori 125–6, 139
How to Be Alone 50, 51
How to Live Together 83
The Human Condition 27, 69

identity 78, 92–3, 95, 122, 139–40
ideology 66, 68
immunity 94
Incel movement 126
indescribable loneliness 4
inter-esse 27, 60
intimacy 15–16, 23–6, 31–2, 34–5, 48, 83, 86, 142, 164–5
isolation 12, 25, 27, 43, 49–51, 56–8, 65–8, 80, 82, 87, 103–4, 116, 121, 127, 137

Jacobs, Jane 132, 147–50
the join 166–7
Journal of a Solitude 58
Julian of Norwich 47

King, Robert 44
Knight, Christopher 45, 48, 49

The Labyrinth of Solitude 33
Laing, Olivia 4
Lane, Melissa 46
Lessing, Doris 81
lone killer 70
loneliness. *See individual entries*
loneliness experts 18–21, 68, 83, 123
"The Loneliness Project" 5

The Lonely City 4
lonely deaths 124, 127
the lonely I 4–5, 20
the lonely we 6–7
long-term care homes 159–60
love 37, 157–8, 161–6
Lucretius 142

McIntosh, Mary 73, 85–7
Maitland, Sara 50–1, 54
Manitoba colony 89, 90, 94, 96
Marantz, Andrew 117
Marcuse, Herbert 69
market 155–6
marriage 18, 72, 76, 77, 87
Marx, Karl 100, 101, 105
May, Rollo 9
meaningfulness 51–2, 70, 73, 104, 106, 119, 137, 157
meaninglessness 69, 105, 110, 125, 127
Melandri, Lea 79
Mennonites 90, 96
mental health 18, 51, 54, 160
Monbiot, George 14, 17
Montaigne, Michel de 164
Morrison, Toni 22, 165
Moustakas, Clark 4, 34, 62
"My Life Is a Joke" 168
The Myth of Sisyphus 112

Nausea 37
needs of the soul 160
neighborhood 139, 147–50
Nietzsche 40
No Exit 84, 136
North Pond Hermit 45

nostalgia 83, 97–9

octogenarians 12
organized loneliness 65–70, 100, 123, 127
The Origins of Totalitarianism 66
Orpheus Descending 33

pandemic pause 131–7
paradox of loneliness 3, 22
"pariah aura of untouchability" 9–10
pathologization of loneliness 14, 18, 21
Paz, Octavio 33
Peplau, Letitia Anne 15
Perlman, Daniel 15
Pinker, Susan 13, 17–20
pluralism 60, 66, 67, 94, 114, 116
Pontellier, Edna 82
prisoners 43–4
private realm 75, 136, 147
proximity 16, 26, 138, 141–5
psychosis 24, 25
public life 66, 67, 69, 87, 136, 148, 152
public realm 26, 115, 136, 151
public toilet analogy 9

Ramanujan, A. K. 138
real loneliness 25
The Rebel 38
recluses 45–7, 125
reclusive religious community 89
Robinson, Marilynne 55

Rodger, Elliot 126
A Room of One's Own 41
Roquentin, Antoine 37

St. Lawrence Market 155–6
Salomé, Lou 40
Samsa, Gregor, alienation of 31–2
Sarton, May 58
Sartre, Jean-Paul 36, 37, 39, 84, 136
Schelling, Friedrich 8
schizophrenic patients 24
self-alienation 62
"Self-Reliance" 40
Sen, Amartya 95
sensory deprivation 43, 50
separateness 33–4, 36, 40, 42, 61, 66
sexual intimacy 34, 142
Shulevitz, Judith 17, 18
sidewalk life 132, 148, 150, 151, 162
Simmel, Georg 145, 146, 152
single mother 80–1
single person 72–9
singlism 78
singularity 60, 144
Sisyphus 37, 38, 134
social care 153
social distancing 132
social failure 124–7
sociality 16, 47, 48, 55, 122
social media 68, 84, 109, 116, 118, 120, 121, 134–5
Sodini, George 127
solidarity 66, 92, 101, 108–9, 122, 123, 132

INDEX

solitary confinement 33, 43, 50, 54, 104, 136
solitude 6, 24–5, 33–5, 41, 57, 58, 80, 134, 137
  ambivalence of 45–55
Solitude: A Return to the Self 51
solus 56–8
Sontag, Susan 32, 58
soul at work 100–11. See also work
Stein, Edith 35, 60, 151
stigma 8–11, 20, 21
Storr, Anthony 48, 51–5, 58, 84, 106
Suarez-Villa, Luis 69, 70, 102
Sullivan, Harry Stack 25
Svendsen, Lars 19, 26, 115

technology 59, 69, 70, 102, 103, 107, 158
  digital 68, 101, 116–18
  iron band 116–23
techno-utopians 117
terror 66, 67, 96
  iron band 116, 122
thinking 53–4
Thoreau, Henry David 6, 46–7, 60
Tillich, Paul 34
Toews, Miriam 89
togetherness 24, 48–9, 54, 60, 62, 67–8, 138, 148, 151
Tönnies, Ferdinand 92

totalitarianism 27, 66, 68, 70, 122
Turkle, Sherry 59
tyranny of the couple 71–9

"The Uncanny" 8
unheimlich 8
"urge to unify" 60

vicarious shame 10
vicissitudes 23, 49, 77, 165
The Village Effect 12, 17
vulnerability 3, 4, 8–10, 35, 40, 54–5, 80, 85, 119, 166

Walden 47
Weil, Simone 160, 161
White, Emily 4
Williams, Tennessee 33
Willis, Paul 46
Women Talking 89
Woolf, Virginia 33, 34, 41
work 52, 56, 69, 73, 78, 100–11, 113–14, 123, 125, 134, 136, 148, 158–9. See also soul at work
workplace loneliness 103
world alienation 69
worldlessness 70, 115, 140
worldliness 13, 26–7, 69, 162

zealot of seriousness 32, 58
Zuboff, Shoshana 70
Zuckerberg, Mark 118

www.ingramcontent.com/pod-product-compliance
Lightning Source LLC
Chambersburg PA
CBHW051643230426
43669CB00013B/2426